GOLF

How to Improve Your Game

GOLF

How to Improve Your Game

Tommy Horton
with Neil Elsey

The Crowood Press

First published in 1988 by
The Crowood Press
Ramsbury, Marlborough,
Wiltshire SN8 2HE

British Library Cataloguing in Publication Data

Horton, Tommy
    Golf: how to improve your game
    1. Golf
    I. Title
    796.352'3   GV965

ISBN 1-85223-102-5

Picture Credits
Fig 8 by Frank Gardner/Golf World; Fig 60 by K.R. Hailey/Hailey
Sports Photographic; Figs 59, 62 and 68 by Stuart Kendall/
Sportsphoto Agency; Figs 39 and 40 by Lawrence Levy/Yours in
Sport; Figs 5 and 6 by Ken Lewis/Sports Photo-Graphics; Figs 7 and
61 by Phil Sheldon (PSPA, NUJ)/Phil Sheldon Photography. All
demonstration photographs by Stuart McAllister (LMPA, LBIPP).

Typeset by Chippendale Type, Otley, West Yorkshire.
Printed in Great Britain by The Bath Press.

Contents

Foreword

Looking back, I believe it would be true to say that Tommy Horton was my first real friend in professional golf. The friendship now extends over 26 years and, during that time, there has been one thing I, and so many others have always admired about him – his utter dedication to his chosen profession. I think if I was asked to encapsulate my thoughts about Tommy in two words, 'completely reliable' would always be the ones to stand out.

Because of that, I know he will have applied himself to this book in the same way he has applied himself throughout his professional career. For, as well as being a successful touring pro, Tommy has been one of only a handful of players able to combine this with the club pro side of golf.

From his early association with Royal Jersey, on to Ham Manor in Sussex and then back to Royal Jersey 12 years ago, Tommy's dual role has meant he is now also regarded as one of our top club professionals with a reputation for easy-to-understand, logical teaching. The success of that can be measured by the fact that many of our young pros joining the circuit have been just as keen as his own club members to seek his advice.

Like myself, Tommy feels a personal responsibility to do his bit for the tour and the administration side of golf. I have admired the way his seemingly ceaseless energy has been put towards improving standards in all quarters of professional golf.

In 1978, during his year of captaincy at the PGA, he led the British and Irish club pros to victory over the United States – thanks for showing me the way, Tommy! For the past 14 years he has been on the PGA European tour tournament committee, and its chairman for the past 3 years. He has also been on the tour board of directors for the same length of time. You therefore won't be surprised to hear that Tommy lists after-dinner speaking and lecturing among his interests.

With World Cup and Ryder Cup honours, plus a string of tour victories throughout the world, Tommy, perhaps more than any other player, has covered the whole spectrum of professional golf. Now all golfers can benefit from his years of experience and, if they follow his advice in these pages, improve their standard of play. Tommy's thoughts on the swing and his teaching methods are sound, simple and, like the man himself, straight down the middle. After reading this fine book, you will learn how to be a better golfer.

Tony Jacklin OBE

Introduction

Having been involved with professional golf for thirty years and the world circuit for over twenty, I feel I have something valuable to offer golfers of all abilities. I have gleaned my golfing knowledge from great men such as Max Faulkner, Jack Nicklaus and the magical Seve Ballesteros, and my association with marvellous teachers such as Henry Cotton and John Jacobs has helped me immensely. I can honestly say I am proud to have learned the golf business from these great golfers.

As a young lad, I learned my golf at Royal Jersey Golf Links, the home of the legendary Harry Vardon. No young man had more incentive to be a great player than I. Jersey golfers were, and still are, enormously proud of Harry Vardon. Of course, I wanted to be the next Vardon and each time I played, I pretended he was watching me. Every shot was important as I wanted to be a worthy successor.

My real playing career, though, started in the early 1960s the same time as Tony Jacklin's. We have been friends ever since. Tony was the 'man to beat' in those early days and soon became an international star. He was our yardstick and we were carried along with his success. During his tour playing days, Tony beat the Americans on his own, and, in more recent years, he captained the first European team to win the Ryder Cup since 1957. Tony made every young British and European professional think that all these things were possible. He did it with a beautiful golf swing and an enormous desire to succeed.

My own playing career has not been quite as successful as Tony Jacklin's, but it's still been good enough to play and win in most golfing countries of the world. It is the knowledge accumulated over this time that I want to share with you.

In my early golfing years I used a long swing with a three to four knuckle left hand grip. It was a hooker's grip, which was certainly the case with me! All my problems were on the left side of the course. My swing certainly kept the ball under the wind, which frequently blew at Royal Jersey, but, as my handicap got lower, I realised that controlling the ball after it landed was just as important as hitting it a long way or low.

While Assistant Pro at the Royal Jersey I was extremely lucky to work for Mr Charles T. Tudor, the Professional. Mr Tudor taught me the almost forgotten art of club making and helped me a great deal with my game giving me lots of time to practise. He also showed me how to 'teach golf'. He would often take me to the practice ground and make bad swings purposely, then ask me what he had done wrong. Because of this sort of instruction I learned to diagnose faults and to teach properly. Sadly, not many pros go to these lengths to teach their assistants, although the Professional Golfers' Association now have extremely good teaching programmes for young men coming into the golf business. Young pros now are far better than they were in my early days.

After two years as assistant to Mr Tudor I was lucky enough to be accepted as Assistant Pro to Mr W.T. Twine at Ham Manor in Angmering, Sussex. This was in 1959 and I felt at the time that I had to leave Jersey to get wider experience before trying my hand on the tournament circuit.

Mr 'Bill' Twine had been a fine player, and a friend and fellow competitor of the great Henry Cotton. I learned not only shop management, but also how to compete in tournaments. Mr Twine made me realise that it was no use trying to play golf in tournaments until I could beat all the Sussex pros. In other words, I was not ready – my golf swing and my mental attitude were not good enough. Whereas in Jersey I had probably been the best player, I was certainly not the best player in Sussex, and Sussex did not at that time have one 'regular' tournament player.

His advice naturally hurt but it had made me even more determined to practise and prove myself. With Mr Twine's help I worked hard and became the best player in Sussex within two years.

However, it was in 1963 that my 'big break' came. I was advised by a good friend of mine that, if I could finish in the first five of the forthcoming Coombe Hill Assistants' tournament he would recommend me to be sponsored by a wealthy London business man. I was lucky again, I tied for fourth! A month later I was interviewed by Mr Ernest Butten and signed up in January 1964 as one of the 'Butten Boys'. There were four Butten Boys at that time, the most famous being Brian Barnes, a great character and a great player.

It was also at this time that I met Max Faulkner. Mr Butten employed Max to teach the Boys to become champions. He was so enthusiastic. We laughed a lot, worked hard and life was absolutely marvellous. We were virtually being paid for doing what we loved most, and were being taught our

Fig 1 The Butten Boys outside the Sundridge Park Management centre, November 1964. Left to right: Tommy Horton, Alan Ibberson, Max Faulkner, Ernest Butten, Iain Clarke, Brian Barnes.

profession by one of our great heroes. They were indeed golden days, and Max improved our techniques as well as made us believe in ourselves. He was an inspiration to all of us.

After two years on the British circuit I started touring deciding to leave the Butten scheme and go it alone. I had a few reasonably successful years on the circuit and then when my former boss Mr Twine decided to retire in 1968, I took over as full Professional at Ham Manor. At the same time I married Helen. The life seemed to agree with me as I soon started winning important tournaments around the world – South Africa, Nigeria, Zambia and, of course, Britain – while still doing the job at Ham Manor. The members were very good, allowing me to play in all the major tournaments. I made a diary of events for each year, so they knew when I would be away, and when I would be at the club and available for teaching. I have always enjoyed teaching, and have many friends who have remained pupils since the early days.

In 1975, my home club – Royal Jersey – asked me to return

to be their Professional. I agreed immediately, as Helen and I now had two small children (Justin and Georgina) and we thought that Jersey would be a marvellous place to bring them up. We have never regretted that decision. I have been very happy at the Royal and even continued to have some playing success – getting into the 1975 and 1977 Ryder Cup Teams. My best ever win, in fact, came a year later when I won the 1978 Dunlop Masters.

In that same year I was made captain of the Professional Golfers' Association, an honour I was extremely proud of. During the autumn of 1978 I started the Young Professional Golfers' School, in Jersey. This was the only school of its kind outside America, and I managed to find sponsors so that it did not cost the young men anything. Fellow professionals like John Stirling, Roger Mace, Dai Rees and John Jacobs came along and gave their advice for free. A doctor friend, who was a very fine player, lectured the young pros on how to keep fit and take care of themselves. Doctor Gracey also taught us positive thinking, and how to practise control of the mind in stressful situations. Finally, Geoffrey Piper, my accountant, lectured us on such matters as how to take care of our finances and how to keep proper accounts of expenses and savings. It is amazing how many sportsmen ignore these details and end up in debt.

These professional schools really made me think more about teaching, and my association with John Jacobs made me realise that very few professionals could actually 'prove' their teaching methods. Many teachers in the past taught 'feelings', or things they had tried successfully themselves. In the properly organised schools run by our PGA now, young professionals learn the basics in far more detail than they ever did. The standard of teaching has risen enormously in recent years because of knowledge passed on by men like John Jacobs, John Stirling and Alex Hay.

Fortunately more people are keen to learn the game properly now than ever before. Even professionals realise they can improve their games too and I frequently have visits in Jersey from tournament pros who need help to regain their form. I thoroughly enjoy working with them, because I realise how hard it is to make a good living on the golf circuits of the world, having travelled myself for over twenty years.

In the following pages of the book I will be advising on the most important ways to move the golf ball in the right direction, and at the correct trajectory. I truly believe that everyone can learn to play golf better. People who believe 'you can't teach an old dog new tricks' are wrong. Any golfer who really wishes to improve can, with sensible teaching and practice, do so. I want to show you how.

Every golfer is different, there are not two swings alike. Although most golfers slice the ball, each player does it in a slightly different way. It is up to the individual to discover why the clubface is open to the swing path at impact, because this is what causes the ball to slice. Very few players pay attention to the actual flight of the ball. Most prefer to either close their stance or even aim further left. This book will teach you how to recognise each curve of the ball. With a little thought you will then be able to alter each stray shot.

All good teachers start with each pupil by checking first the clubface at address, then the grip or hold of the club. Next comes the width and direction of the stance. Lastly, the posture – vital for the correct shoulder turn and good balance. Whether teaching a beginner or a top-class player these are the starting points. Check these with me and I guarantee you too can improve.

1   The Right Equipment

The very best players go to great lengths to choose their own clubs. Quite often you will find odd clubs in a great golfer's bag. Normally these odd clubs will be drivers, wedges and putters. In every case they will be the favourites of that player. Driving may be for show and not for 'dough', but it is virtually impossible to set up great birdie chances if the drive has been hit into heavy rough, or even out of bounds. Driving is a very necessary part of playing confident and consistent golf.

If professionals go to such lengths in selecting important clubs it is even more important for the average player who does not have time to spend trying out dozens of new clubs. 'Professionals can hit the ball with any sort of club,' I am often told. That is only partly true. They can hit the ball with anything, but they cannot perform to their optimum ability unless they use equipment which suits them perfectly.

The foolproof way to find equipment which suits you, is to put your trust in your local pro. Ask him, first, if he can recommend a certain brand of club, and then which shaft, weight and grip size will suit you. If he shows genuine interest in your request, next ask if he will allow you to try two or three of his different types of club. A 5- or 6-iron from each set will give a good indication of how the set plays and feels. After five or ten shots with each club a definite pattern will emerge. At least one of the clubs will feel good and will strike the ball differently and better than the others.

I like to go to the practice ground with my clients to make sure they are swinging well and trying the clubs intelligently. This is the sort of thing you cannot do if buying equipment in a high street discount store. It does not matter how much you pay for your clubs. It will be a waste of money if they do not suit you.

Shafts and Weight

Today's modern equipment is far superior to anything we have had before. My first club was a cumbersome, hickory-

Fig 2   The complete set of golf clubs.

shafted mashie. The shaft was bent and heavier than the clubhead. The modern trend is to find the lightest possible material for shafts, so the head weight can be increased. This makes sense as it is only the clubhead which hits the ball. Over the years we have discovered that a certain overall weight of club can be swung by the average player most efficiently. If that weight can be taken out of the shaft and put into the clubhead, we produce our best results.

Ladies cannot swing the longer, heavier clubs which most men use. Ladies' clubs are therefore lighter, shorter, and need thinner grips as they have smaller hands. Large women can manage gents' clubs if they are also strong but I usually recommend slightly longer, ladies' clubs for the larger women I teach, varying the grip thickness to suit each client. (The longer shaft also makes them feel heavier – the clubs that is!)

I do not recommend smaller women to have normal ladies' clubs cut shorter, as these ladies do not usually hit the ball very far. Instead, I flatten the lie of the normal length clubs which helps them hit the ball correctly and retains the wide arc given by this type of club. A narrow arc, produced by a short club, makes long shots almost impossible. Many good pros prefer their clubs to be longer than standard and their short irons (wedge and sand irons) flatter than standard. The flatter lie makes them more manageable for the pitch and chip shots. The normal rule is – flat lying clubs for short people, and upright for tall golfers. This principle naturally applies to men as well.

Golfers with weak hands, who do not hit the ball very far, should strive to use the lightest shafts possible and, to some extent, lighter heads too. This type of player does not hit the ball great distances and needs more clubhead speed. A double-handed or baseball grip could also help to generate this. Of the two types of metal used for iron clubs, short hitters would be well advised to use the *cast* steel type as the ball does fly off faster from this metal, than from *mild* steel.

While on the subject of the short hitters – golf balls are very different now too. If distance is the problem the *solid* golf ball does fly off the club faster and runs further. Do remember though, that the conventional *wound* ball does normally fly through the air further, and stops more quickly on landing. It also marks or cuts more easily.

The choice of equipment is a very important part of improving one's golf. Some clubs are designed to hit the ball high and some to hit it low. These different clubs can be used to suit a particular player's preferred shot.

The flex of the shaft is not quite as important as it was when we all used heavier shafts. However, because shafts are much lighter now, we tend to keep the flex range smaller. We only used whippier shafts, for ladies or short hitters, to increase clubhead speed and we now achieve that with the lighter shafts.

Junior Clubs

Parents of juniors would be well advised to obtain advice from a good pro when thinking about clubs for their children. Guard against giving children 'dad's old clubs'. These would be far too heavy and too long, and would make it practically impossible for the child to use a proper swing.

For children aged between six and nine years of age it is now possible to buy 'junior' clubs. These are made with small heads, with whippy and much shorter shafts. They are properly balanced and can be used very successfully. Older children, up to early teenagers, should use women's clubs, shortened to suit their height. Women's clubs have slightly larger heads and shafts than junior clubs.

Attention must be given to the thickness of the grips of these junior clubs. Remember that a child's hand is nowhere near as large as an adult's. In most cases junior clubs should be fitted with leather grips, as these can be tailor-made for the child. The average rubber grip, on even a lady's club, will be far too thick for a junior player. As the hold on the club is of paramount importance do not overlook these things. Children will not learn the correct swing if they cannot hold the club correctly. Take good care to fit the clubs for your children otherwise they may develop unusual swing actions from their early learning days, which could stay with them all their golfing lives. It is an absolute joy to see properly taught children play golf. They are so supple and enthusiastic that we owe them a good start in their golfing lives.

Normal length women's clubs are perfect for middle teenagers as at that age they are just strong enough to swing them properly. Clubs must be manageable. Heavy clubs are completely unmanageable and dangerous for the weaker player.

Of course, it's not necessary to buy new equipment. Most professionals take in second-hand clubs in part exchange so they can often find clubs to suit young players at a reasonable price.

Loft and Lie

Apart from altering the thickness of grips, lengths of shafts and leading edges of iron clubs, it is also important to play with clubs which lie correctly. Clubs which are too upright make a golfer pull the ball to the left (for right-handers) and those which are too flat make the golfer slice or hit the ball to the right.

Most iron clubs can be altered quite easily particularly if they are made of mild steel. Cast steel is naturally more brittle so care is essential when altering them. Remember too that mild steel irons do impart more backspin and generally give slightly more control. Cast clubs do not spin the ball quite as much and are extremely popular with golfers who do not hit the ball very far. Top class amateurs and professionals generally prefer the feel and control that mild steel clubs produce, whereas ladies and shorter-hitting people prefer the benefit of the extra length they acquire from cast steel.

Those players who find real difficulty in using long irons (4, 3 or even 2 irons) should experiment with 5 or even 6 or 7 woods. I even know players who use a number 9 wood

Fig 3   (a) When the heel of the club is off the ground as much as it is here, the club is far too flat.

(b) This club is too upright, as only the heel is touching the grass.

(c) This is the correct lie for the golf club, with only a small part of the toe off the ground.

extremely effectively. Naturally, the extra loft on these woods enables the player to get the ball airborne quickly, and the fairly long shaft helps to hit the golf ball good distances. A 5 wood, for instance, should hit the ball about as far as a number 3 iron, while the 7 wood hits about as far as the 4 or 5 iron. The 9 wood is about the same as a 6 or 7 iron.

The only instant cures I have any faith in are for those players who either hit the ball too low or too high. Of course this is normally due to a faulty swing or a poor hold of the club, but clubs can have the loft removed or increased by any competent professional. It is even possible to buy ones designed to hit the ball higher. These usually have more weight in the sole.

Many clubs are designed with the leading edge of the clubface forward of the shaft, and these do tend to hit the ball higher as they contact the ball before the hands and arms pass the ball. The offset club naturally has the reverse effect, and has been the fashion in recent years. Most of the more popular putters are in fact offset. This is because players like to feel their hands ahead of the ball for short chips and particularly on putts.

If you use clubs which are too upright your shots will tend to fly to the left consistently. This is caused by the heel of the club making contact with the ground, which tends to close the face at impact. Clubs which are too flat tend to make a player slice as the toe hits the ground and opens on impact.

It is well worth checking your clubs every few months as strong players can shift the loft and lie, particularly on firm ground or even on those awful mats that some clubs use in the wet, winter months. I have often checked sets with three clubs having the same loft! The whole idea of a matched set is that all the angles are regular so that the same swing can be used for each club.

All these points are well worth considering for every type of golfer. A full set of clubs is expensive, so look for a helpful pro who will find you a set to suit your swing. Don't just buy a set because your pals are playing well with a certain type of club. Always try them out first. Remember, too, that thickness of grip is important. Basically thin grips make the hands more active during the golf swing; while thick grips tend to deaden the hands and wrists, so eliminating feel. It is essential to have feel through your hands during the swing, as they are the only link between your body and that all-important golf club. 'No feel' brings 'no confidence' so consider those hands when buying new clubs. Also, don't forget to wash the old grips on your clubs as slippery grips are often the cause of inconsistency.

Fig 4 This clearly indicates the difference between an offset club (left) and the conventional clubhead (right). The leading edge of the offset model is behind the shaft of the club, but the leading edge of the conventional club is level with the shaft.

16

Maintaining your Equipment

Very few golfers take real care of their equipment. Clubs are thrown into the boot of the car, dirty and often wet, until the next game. Sweaters and waterproofs are screwed up and stuffed into pockets of golf bags and shoes are thrown dirty and wet into damp lockers. This is fine for club pros, as the equipment soon wears out anyway, and we just replace it! But if you do manage to find a nice set of clubs and some really good equipment, make the effort to preserve it. If it is expensive and you enjoy using it, look after it. If you don't have time to do that, ask your Assistant Pro to do it for you and negotiate a servicing price.

In years to come the Pro and his assistants will be employed to do more and more in our golf clubs. They are being trained to give advice in far more departments of the golf business, so don't be frightened to ask their advice. Your club pays him a retainer for his expertise so make use of him. Become one of the regulars, and you will be amazed at how much free and friendly information you will receive.

2   Good Technique

Usually, the best players have the best techniques, although this does not mean they necessarily have the best looking swings. I am often told, especially by women, that a certain lady has a very pretty swing but has a very high handicap. Many children too, look good, or have good-looking swings, but do not play particularly well. There is a very good reason for these observations. Most supple or loose-limbed players, like women or children, move their bodies and legs in a flowing manner, but actually do not control the movement of the club very well. Hence the good, flowing look – but not necessarily good technique!

Occasionally, an uncomfortable or awkward-looking player, like Lee Trevino, comes along to prove the purists wrong. However, Trevino, in the eyes of many professionals, is technically very good. His swing is fairly short, but it is consistent. In other words, he is in full control of his abbreviated movements.

Good technique simply means that the very necessary *body movements* a player has to make during the swing, must co-ordinate with the arm and club movements. What this means is as follows: the shoulders and hips turn out of the way on the backswing to allow the club and arms to swing upwards; the weight shifts on to the left side on the downswing as the arms swing the club towards the ball; finally, the swing is only completed when the left side (hips and shoulders) turn out of the way and the club and arms are allowed to swing up again to a full follow-through. Only the very best players learn the knack of co-ordinating these most important movements consistently – other players do it occasionally. Co-ordination can, however, be obtained by practice. In saying that, most golfers fall into one of two categories. They either use too much body action, particularly on the downswing; or too much arm action, without shifting their weight correctly. Slicers usually throw their bodies into the shot, leaving the clubhead behind and too open. Players who hook usually do not move the body very much on the downswing but deliver the clubhead early, causing it to close and send the ball flying to the left.

Fig 5   (right) Seve Ballesteros. An incredible photograph of the classic golf swing – perfectly poised, but completely wound up. This is an extremely powerful position that only the young can achieve.

Fig 6   (overleaf) The golf swing that has won Jack Nicklaus more major titles than any other player in the history of golf. Although a strong position, this swing could be achieved by any player. Perhaps a little more knee action than I would prefer, but a wonderful arc and club position.

Fig 7   (overleaf right) The unique flying elbow of Eamonn Darcy. His left-hand grip is weak at address, and his right hand lets go at the top of the backswing. All these things equal out at impact, and make Eamonn a regular winner on the world circuits.

18

Great players, like Severiano Ballesteros, spend hours trying to obtain the timing of these movements. At any of the major events he can be seen making dozens of practice swings, even during a round. Most of these great players call this 'timing'. In fact it's the 'feeling' of when to deliver the final hit or acceleration of the club on the downswing. When this technique is achieved, the player's confidence grows and success comes naturally.

I believe that the correct swing, or a consistent swing, must be achieved before any confidence can last. A good technique can be taught by experienced teachers, providing the pupil is prepared to work at the basic principles. Ben Hogan once said 'Any golfer who is prepared to learn the correct grip, will be rewarded a thousand times over.' This is indeed marvellous advice. Practice is only exercise if you don't have a sound method. Have a picture of the correct swing in your mind when practising and get someone to check your swing occasionally. Any adjustment must be done slowly because it will feel strange. Do these things gradually and learn proper control. Good technique can only be achieved by slowly building up the correct movements. If a slow swing is practised often enough, the proper action will eventually be incorporated into the normal swing.

'Technique' in golf simply means that the golf club is held properly, the stance and posture are not exaggerated, and the club is swung into position at the top of the backswing so that the correct angles are achieved. Thus the sequence is:

1. The club is parallel to the ground with the clubhead in a neutral position.
2. The shaft is aimed directly at the target.
3. The shoulders and hips are properly turned.

Technique on the downswing combines the right amount of weight shift with the correct square delivery of the all-important clubhead. The follow-through is simply the correct positioning of the body which allows the arms and the club to continue on to a well balanced high finish.

Most golfers recognise the great techniques of the top players but lack it themselves because they fail to carry out one or two of the most important fundamentals of the set-up and swing.

Fig 8 (left) Lee Trevino's swing is quite short, a little flat, and he aims left of the target; but just before impact everything falls into place, and his record shows that he knows exactly what is happening.

3 The Grip

My first introduction to the learning process of golf started at school when I found Tommy Armour's book *How to play your best golf all the time.* In that book, and every other golf instruction book I have ever read, the authors have stressed the importance of holding the club properly. Sadly, with all this knowledge available, the ways most amateur golfers hold the club never cease to surprise me. My own opinion is that nothing is more important than learning the correct way to grip the club – without this, the correct swing becomes impossible.

The best advice I can give any would-be golfer, is to have a few lessons before even attempting to hit the golf ball. All pros realise the importance of a good grip and can help future players enjoy the game even more, in the knowledge that they have started properly and have a real chance of becoming a sound player.

The entire golf swing depends on having both hands in a strictly neutral position, so that neither hand overpowers the other during the backswing or downswing. Both hands *must* work together at all times. Very few amateur golfers appreciate the importance of this harmony of the hands until it is too late, so absolute beginners would be well advised to learn to hold the club comfortably and correctly before they try to hit the ball.

Nearly all players who hold the club well, swing the club well. Poor swings are usually a result of compensating for a poor hold of the club. Visit a major tournament and watch the great players. Their hands seem a part of their clubs, and give perfect co-ordination with their other movements.

Vardon, Interlocking and Baseball Grips

The correct grip can be achieved in three basic ways. The most popular way to hold the club is the Vardon grip. This involves placing the left hand on the club (for right-handed players) approximately one inch from the top of the shaft, with the left thumb pointing down towards the clubhead. On

 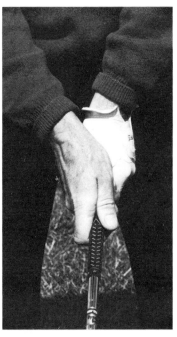 

Fig 9   The correct position for the left hand.

Fig 10   Both hands folded properly around the clubshaft.

Fig 11   This is an unusual photograph, but shows the golfer's correct hand position. With this grip both hands work together.

looking down at the left hand, two or three knuckles should be visible – two for strong men, three for women. The club should be held mainly in the fingers with no gap between the little finger and the shaft. Grip pressure should be shared equally by all the fingers. The next move is to place the right hand below the left, with the right thumb this time on the left side of the shaft. The little finger of the right hand must overlap, or be placed on top of, the index finger of the left hand.

When this process has been followed, the golfer will notice that the palms of both hands actually face each other, and the back of the left hand, and palm of the right, face the intended target. The left thumb should fit snugly into the palm of the right hand and the two 'V's, formed between thumbs and forefingers, will now point to the right shoulder.

Naturally, with new players, this hold will feel most unusual and uncomfortable, particularly if the grip is too tight. The secret is to hold the club quite loosely, until it becomes comfortable. Experienced players, who have to change their grip, will also find the change much easier to live with if they do not hold too tightly for the first few days. Only hold the club tightly enough to stop it moving during the swing.

The 'interlocking' hold of the club is only slightly different from the Vardon grip, in that the right little finger intertwines with the left forefinger. The palms still face each other, and from the front view it looks the same. The rule of two or three knuckles of the left hand still applies, and the 'V's formed between index fingers and thumbs should point towards the right shoulder.

The third way looks the same from the front view also, but involves both hands being placed on the club separately and as close together as possible. This is commonly known as the 'baseball' grip and is normally taught to women, children or men with small or weak hands. Because the hands are slightly apart, this enables golfers to use extra leverage to accelerate the clubhead. Again the palms should face each other, and 'V's should point to the right shoulder.

Whatever hold you prefer to use, do remember that before the hands are placed on the club, the clubface must be lined up correctly with the target. Place the sole of the club flat on the ground, and the leading edge at right angles to the intended line. Many players are guilty of placing the hands on the club before lining it up correctly.

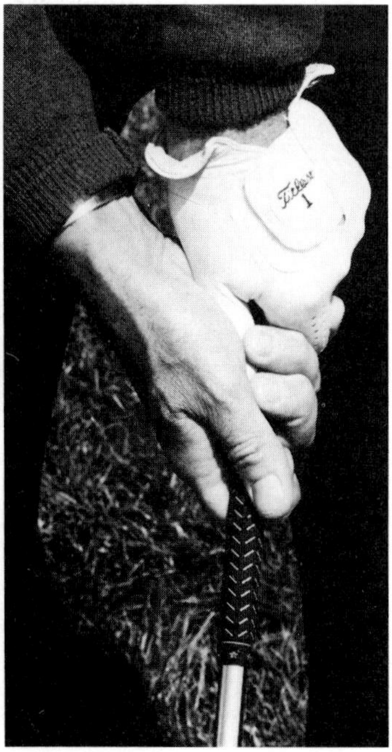

Compensating for Faults

Golfers who adopt a strong or hooker's grip naturally have to compensate during the swing by adopting a slicer's action. Others, who use a weak or slicer's grip, conversely, have to adopt a hooker's type of swing. One glance from an experienced professional puts certain players in either the slicer or hooker category.

Apart from the normal grip changes (strong to neutral or weak to neutral) the following are not commonly known. Good players often find that a minor adjustment, like 'shortening' their left thumb can make the hands more active during the swing. This adjustment is recommended frequently for players who tend to slice. It enables them to use the club more on the downswing which, in turn, squares the clubhead before impact. Most slicers leave the clubhead open too long on the downswing.

The reverse can be advised for players who hook the ball a

Fig 12   Both hands are too far under, on the right-hand side of the shaft. Commonly known as the hooker's grip, this is a favourite of beginners, but it is quite wrong.

little too much. These players frequently use excessive hand action on the downswing and close the clubface too early. By lengthening the left thumb, or stretching it, down the top of the shaft, the left wrist becomes firmer and restricts the use of the hands. Another interesting way to stop the hands taking over is to hold firmly with the right hand, particularly with the middle two fingers and the thumb. This exercise stops the right hand opening and becoming too active during the swing.

Generally, I do not approve of too many independent changes, but these minor adjustments are invaluable when actually competing during a tournament round. Another thing worth noting is that very active hands and wrists tend to close the clubface, and stiff wrists promote pushing or slicing.

The ultimate, of course, is to grip with the same pressure from both hands so that they deliver the blow with equal force at the right time. A note of warning here to fairly seasoned players whose game is stagnant and cannot make further progress. Look no further than the set-up, and your grip of the golf club. It is virtually impossible to continue improvement unless these address checks are followed properly.

I like to spend the entire first lesson with an absolute beginner, just getting them used to holding the club, gently swinging it up and down with a half swing, until it feels comfortable and strong in both hands. The second lesson is spent addressing the ball correctly and cultivating a comfortable and accurate backswing. Achieving a good position at the top of the backswing is the next piece in the puzzle. With these two pieces well practised and consistent the main set-up has been achieved. From here on it is to a certain extent, instinct, for no two players swing the club in the same way or with the same speed.

I always spend more time on the above preparation, as most beginners seem in a great hurry to hit dozens of balls as soon as possible. One hour in a golfer's life is *nothing* in terms of the time he will spend on the course; but at the start of his golfing life it means *everything*.

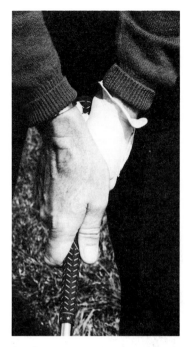

Fig 13 A real slicer's grip – with the hands far too much on top of, or too far to the left of, the shaft.

4 Setting-up to the Ball

The 'set-up', which includes posture, is another part of golf that is very easy to achieve; yet only a few players take the trouble to follow the basic rules. These simple rules are, stand tall, with the back straight, the legs slightly bent and the feet square to the target, about shoulder width apart. One normally finds that a player who walks with a long, loping stride, will adopt a wide stance when playing golf. Of course, the reverse is also the case. A person who takes small steps usually plays golf with a narrow stance. The reason for this is that they have found their own point of balance in walking, and use the same point of balance for any other activity. Variations are permissible in golf, like anything else, but only slight deviations from the basics are sensible for consistency.

After taking hold of the club and adopting this tall posture, with the back fairly straight, and the head high, gently lower the club to the ball – flexing the knees, and bending the back forward, so the club rests on the grass behind the ball.

I always recommend that the feet, hips and shoulders should be in line with – or square to – the target, fairway or flag, depending on which shot is being played. This applies to nearly every long shot in golf.

Many good players allow their left foot to open or point outwards at the address position. This does, however, restrict the backswing and is only recommended for supple players. Allowing the left foot to point outwards does assist the body to turn through. As mentioned earlier, slight variations are permissible as long as they are indeed *slight*.

Study the top and bottom edges of your clubs. Many people close the clubface because they aim the top edge of their iron clubs. If you look you will see that the edges of the clubhead are at different angles. The correct edge to aim at the target is the bottom of the club. If the top edge is aimed, the ball will almost certainly fly to the left. The reason for this, is that it is the leading (or bottom) edge which strikes the ball first, and obviously affects the ball immediately on contact. So always aim the clubface carefully with the bottom edge aimed squarely at the target and flat on the ground. Watch a good pro prepare for each shot and copy him.

Fig 14   From this view the ball is seen to be played from well inside the left heel. The arms and club form a good triangle; the left arm and clubshaft are almost in line.

28

Fig 15 Note the clubs that are lying on the ground. They indicate the direction of the intended target, and both feet are parallel to them. Also note the posture – with the knees slightly flexed, but the back still fairly straight. The head is held high and not tucked into the chest.

Fig 16 This shows the most common stance in golf, with the feet and shoulders aiming to the left – causing the player to swing the club outside on the backswing, and across the line on the downswing and follow-through.

Fig 17 The less-common hooker's stance, where the right foot and right side are both turned to the right. This causes the club to swing far too much on the inside plane, and return past the ball on the outside arc.

Care, too, must be given to the actual position of the ball at address. For wooden club shots, particularly with the driver, the ball should be positioned opposite the inside of the left foot. This position hardly varies with good players, so it is worth getting right at the very start. For the middle irons, position the ball midway between the feet; and for the shorter irons, slightly back of centre.

In finding these important address positions, be extremely careful to keep the hips and shoulders square to the target line. It is easy to allow the head and shoulders to aim to the left, so get the feeling of staying behind the ball. I mention the head moving forward, as nearly all great players make a conscious effort to move the head slightly to the right of the ball. The great Jack Nicklaus is a perfect example of this. He makes a deliberate effort to move his chin towards his right shoulder, before starting his backswing. This helps his swing to follow the correct path on the backswing and downswing.

Once this address position has been found, check the hand and ball positions. If a line is taken from the clubhead, on up the shaft, the hands should be about level with the navel.

I have heard good players recommend that the hands should be set ahead of the ball, but this changes the position of the clubhead behind it, and can cause other complications which I will discuss at a later stage. Quite simply, aim the clubhead at the target, and the shaft at your navel. This will ensure the correct aim and positioning.

Just follow Sandy Lyle's advice: 'You can slave away for as long as you like on the practice ground, bashing balls, but it all boils down in the end to realising that the set-up makes or ruins nearly every shot you are likely to hit.' This is indeed good advice from one of our best players who does, himself, have trouble at times with his set-up. In fact, whenever good players have trouble with their game they seek advice from friends and fellow competitors, and the most consistent error usually is found in their set-up. The golf swing only changes when the aim changes.

Whilst setting-up, it is better to keep the overall weight on the heels of the feet rather than on the toes. This helps the body turn rather than topple over as one would if the weight were on the toes. It also keeps the golf club on the inside path on the backswing which we all know is the correct swing line.

5 A Better Backswing

Apart from the address position, the backswing should be the easiest part of the swing. Its function is to move the golf club easily and smoothly away from the ball in a wide, *constant* arc, until the shaft is parallel to the ground and is aiming along the line of the intended flight of the ball.

Very few golfers actually start out with this idea in mind. Instead, they try to move the club away from the ball in a low, straight line, without turning the shoulders or hips. This, of course, produces a sway or tilt, apart from moving the head during the swing.

The club, hands, arms and body, should move together in a single action, to co-ordinate the correct turn necessary to get the club in the proper position at the top. If the right side turns away from the ball correctly, the head stays still and consistency can be achieved.

Many golfers worry about when the wrists should cock, or turn. My advice is never to try to cock the wrists – simply allow them to move, by aiming the club at the target, on approaching the top of the backswing. There should be no conscious loosening of the wrists during this action. It should feel as if the arms, and not the wrists, swing the club back, and up, from the ball. Arms keep the arc constant and wide, not wrists. An excessive wrist action changes the angle and direction of the clubface.

While the club and body are being turned, the knees and legs should remain relaxed, so that they are both moved when the right side of the body turns away from the ball. The action of the right hip and shoulder turning, should pull the left knee, hip and shoulder automatically round. The amount the left foot and knee moves, depends entirely on the suppleness of the player. Rotund players usually move their feet and knees more than supple, slender ones. Good players never allow the legs to dominate the movement, particularly on the backswing.

The correct sequence, therefore, involves the body (mainly the right upper half) turning to make room for the club and arms to swing upwards. A flat shoulder turn combined with a high arm action brings the best results.

Fig 18 This clearly shows the shoulders and hips turning out of the way to make room for the arms and club to swing up.

31

Fig 19   The top of my backswing, showing the body fully coiled, the left heel only slightly off the ground, and the clubshaft almost parallel with the ground.

To answer questions on whether the backswing should be upright or flat, inside or straight back, I believe the arm action on the backswing should be upright but wide. The left arm being straight all the way back keeps the arc constant and wide enough without forcing it to be wider. The shoulder action is the flat part of the backswing. This will happen only if the player does not lean over the ball too much. If the posture is good and the back fairly straight, the shoulders turn (flat) as the arms swing up (upright). If these rules are followed the golf club naturally swings away from the ball on a slightly inside plane.

Most great players believe that there should be no real tension on the backswing. The left arm should be comfortably straight. The feeling should be of a high arm action, but on the inside swing path. This combines power with accuracy – we could all do with more of both. Setting the club in the right position enables every golfer to achieve their greatest potential.

6 Improve Your Downswing

Most teachers agree that the downswing starts with the movement of weight back on to the left side although many amateur golfers may not agree. Photographs show that the hips initiate the downswing, as they unwind.

As the hips return to square, the arms start their downward movement before the shoulders start their journey back to the square to target line. The arms can produce a great deal of clubhead speed as the right arm straightens towards impact.

The object of the downswing is to return your body, and the club, back to the same position as before the backswing began. Try to do this in slow motion, for a while, then gradually build up the speed. This is a great way to practise the correct 'squaring up' action of the downswing.

The old 'late hit' advice, has damaged more golf swings than anything else. Late means exactly that – too late! I agree with the saying 'What is wrong with being a little early,' or even better still, on time? Late hitting is caused by the body racing the arms and the club to the ball during the downswing. I prefer to hit 'on time', meaning the body and arms delivering the blow together.

Few players realise that the backswing and downswing planes are not the same. We do try to keep them the same, but because the weight changes during the backswing and downswing these swing paths differ. In general, really good players drop their arms and the club on the 'inside plane' on the way back to the ball. Poor players, and beginners in particular, do the reverse. Their plane is often quite good on the backswing but very much on the outside on the downswing. This usually is because the body races the club which, in turn, is delivered too late. As soon as the clubhead is delivered on time, the right side should move past the ball as the left side clears, allowing the club and arms to drive towards the target.

As we all know, the right arm folds and the right elbow tends to point to the ground on the backswing; but on returning to the ball, or during the downswing, the right arm

Fig 20 (left) This clearly shows the key point in the downswing. This first movement settles the weight to the left, and brings the legs into the same position as at address. This, in turn, drags the arms into the classic hitting position.

Fig 21 (right) This is the moment when it all happens. The club has been swung down, slightly on the inside path. As the club approaches the ball, the right knee kicks forward, and the left side starts to turn out of the way to make room for the follow-through.

must straighten. This straightening action actually helps square up the clubface, and also accelerates it. Very few golfers, even the better ones, talk about the right arm function during the swing, but this is usually the right-hander's strongest arm and must be used. Many players feel that the left arm is the key. After all, it certainly stays fairly straight on the backswing and downswing, keeping the arc constant but the weakest arm must not be the dominant one. Quite simply, the left arm guides the club by staying straight, but the right side and arm deliver the power. The modern saying amongst the world's great players is now, 'You cannot hit too early, if you shift your weight first, on the downswing.' Try it, it really does work.

The ultimate, though, for everyone is to use everything – both feet, legs, arms and hands, all have a part to play, and it's an equal part. Do not take on passengers. They all have a job to do.

Follow-through

At impact, the club and body position should be roughly the same as it was at address. To aid the follow-through, the right knee must kick in towards the left, at the same time as the left side (in particular the left hip) turns away from the target line. This turning away enables the club and arms to accelerate down the target line and on to a fairly high finish. There should be no real conscious effort to glue the head down after hitting the ball. As the club and body turn away after impact the head will follow into a position which will make watching the flight of the golf ball quite natural.

An effort should be made to drive the clubhead down the line to the target after impact. This action starts the ball on the intended line and assures a good contact.

I always encourage my pupils to practise their finishing position as this is an excellent exercise for achieving good balance. A swing with good balance, is a safe and consistent one. Get used to finishing in the same position with every long shot. We all practise our backswings a great deal but few players think of making a proper balanced follow-through. Make a point of practising the complete swing and learn true consistency.

Fig 22   A comfortable relaxed follow-through, with the right heel fully off the ground, left leg firm, and the hands finishing at head height. The eyes have followed the ball, showing that it is not necessary to glue the head down after impact.

7 Selecting the Club

Before playing consistently, every player must practise enough to develop that consistency. The player must know, for instance, how far he hits with each club in the bag. Sadly, few players are really honest with themselves when it comes to distances. Over eighty-five per cent of approaches played to the flagstick fall short. This even applies to chips and putts. I always enjoyed watching Arnold Palmer in his heyday. He attacked the hole whenever he was within range. Of the present-day players Seve Ballesteros is the most exciting, because he attacks most of the time. If it is possible to reach the hole, at least give it a chance.

To compete successfully, you must know roughly how far you hit the ball. The average male golfer hits a drive around 190 yards, his 3-iron about 160, and his pitching wedge 80 yards.

Women, generally, do not hit the ball as far as men, although I have met some women who do. Students will notice that whereas men vary about ten yards per club, women average about eight or nine yards.

One useful thing to remember, is it is more sensible to 'ease up' and take one club more for an approach shot than to try and 'stretch' a club which will reach the target only with a perfect strike.

Fig 23   The approximate distances hit by a wedge, 5-iron, and driver showing the relative run of the ball on landing (the true trajectory is not shown).

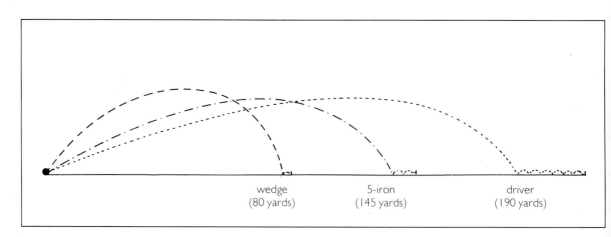

wedge
(80 yards)

5-iron
(145 yards)

driver
(190 yards)

Happily, many golf clubs supply or sell yardage charts for visiting players, so it is worth obtaining one of these before playing a strange course. If you know how far you hit each club, then club selection will no longer be a problem. I advise every golfer to carry one of these charts even on their own course. It is amazing to me, that players still make these simple distance errors even at their own club. Follow this advice and your scores will improve, even if you do not improve your swing.

8 Playing the Shots

Driving is the real joy of golf, because it's the driver that hits the ball the longest distance. However, although hitting the ball as far as possible is the aim of all beginners, after playing the game properly for some time, players soon realise that accuracy is just as important.

Fortunately the ball may be teed up for a drive, and the height of the teed ball varies according to the driver's face depth. It has been the fashion in recent years to have very shallow woods and irons, but I am pleased to see that designs for the latest woods in particular are returning to deeper or larger heads. With very shallow clubheads, it is too easy to swing right under the ball and 'sky' it.

The ideal driver for a middle- or long-handicap player, is a deep-faced, but fairly lofted club. This gives lots of face to hit the ball with, and lots of loft to help get it airborne. A large head usually breeds confidence too. Many golfers find difficulty in hitting a driver because of the lack of loft on the clubface. Any sensible golf pro can properly advise a player on which club would be suitable, as we all know the problems golfers face.

When teeing the ball up, make sure that about half of it is above the top edge of the clubface. This will give it the correct trajectory. Golfers who hook the ball can tee it slightly higher, as a hooked ball usually flies lower.

For a drive, the ball should be teed just opposite the inside of the left foot. Only slight variations should be allowed, as the ball must be struck slightly on the upswing, for a full-blooded drive. Just because a driver hits the longest distance, it does not mean that the player should swing faster, or hit harder. The club itself is larger, which guarantees a wider arc for the swing, and it has less loft than any other club. These two reasons alone make the ball go further than any other golf shot, so do not try to squeeze those extra yards out of the club. Just follow the simple rules I have described in this book and you will be rewarded. A full shoulder turn and a full follow-through are essential.

Wooden club shots from the fairway, or even the light rough, only present a problem to golfers who hook the ball, or those who adopt a 'hooker's grip' (right hand under the shaft, or three or four knuckles showing on the left hand). Only players with a poor hold of the club find fairway woods a problem. Of course, beginners find them difficult, too, and would be well advised to use a number 3 wood from the tee. A number 3 or even 4 wood is easier to use from the tee than the driver and far more consistent. It's worth losing a few yards, when one considers the consistency factor. Confidence plays a large part in golf and the easier you make the game by clever thinking, the sooner you will improve.

Long irons are a favourite with many good players, and invaluable to most professionals, but often a nuisance to less competent golfers. Due to their lack of loft and the small head, naturally, only a shot hit in the middle of the club gives the maximum benefit. Most players find they hit the ball just as far with a 4-iron as they do with a 2-or 3-iron so they prefer to use a number 4 or 5 wood instead.

It is important to make a full shoulder turn, and a high arm and club action to hit long irons. The correct arc and angle of the club must be maintained to obtain maximum benefit. A long sweeping action, similar to that for fairway woods produces the best results. A steep, chopping action must be avoided.

Mid-irons (5, 6 or 7) are the favourites of most golfers and are usually the clubs that players start learning with. Most professionals teach beginners with a 6- or 7-iron because these clubs have a generous face area and enough loft to get the ball airborne, even if it is not hit from the middle of the clubface. Another reassuring thing about the mid-irons is the comfortable shaft length. A 6- or a 7-iron is a very forgiving club.

As it is important to keep accuracy in mind for these clubs, a three-quarter swing is all that is necessary. A fairly full shoulder turn, with a slightly open stance, keeps the backswing in the correct position and aids a slightly sharper descent of the downswing. The sharper descent enables you to control the ball on landing. When the ball is struck with a descending blow, more backspin is imparted. This is why the ball stops more quickly on landing. This sharper descent is caused by the weight shifting forward and slightly across the target line.

Fig 24   This shows the various positions from which the clubs are played. Note the distances that these clubs are from the feet. The clubs shown are (front to back): the driver; the 3-iron; the 7-iron and the wedge.

Short iron shots are often the key to good scoring. Accuracy is essential with these shots, as most players hit more of these than any other, whether they be full 8- or 9-iron shots or the most used club in the bag, the pitching wedge. The wedge can be used for shots of up to 110 yards or down to 20 or 30 yards. More shots are saved or lost by using this club than almost any other shot in golf.

Many golfers feel they have to use a scooping action when playing a half wedge or pitch. Nothing is further from the truth. The wedge has up to 55° loft and that is more than enough for any normal short shot. A slightly open stance and a full arm action will loft the ball with great accuracy and consistency. Anyone who learns to use this club well, will be admired by golfers everywhere. Again, use a three-quarter backswing, mainly with the arms, shift the weight to the left side, and completely control the follow-through without forcing it.

9 Understanding Ball Flight

Any player who wishes to control the golf ball, must first understand exactly what the ball does when struck in certain ways by the clubhead.

The diagrams overleaf show exactly what sort of spin is imparted when the clubhead approaches the ball from certain directions and angles. Every player should familiarise themselves with these effects.

My impression is that very few players understand these principles – certainly, few practise them. When I teach people these things, I frequently get blank looks of amazement as if all is finally being revealed. Too many golfers think there is some little trick or gimmick that they are going to find, to improve their game. If a player has a definite pattern to his game, whether it is a slice or hook, improvement is simple. It is when players hit an enormous variety of shots successively that teachers have problems. That is why pros like to start beginners from scratch. This way the pupil does not start with any bad habits.

The perfect arc for the clubhead is on a very slight curve, because the player stands to the side of the ball. (The arc would be straight up and down, like a pendulum, if the player were directly over the ball.) The curve is created because of the shoulders and body turn during the swing. This arc is described as 'in' during the backswing, 'square' at impact and 'in' on the follow-through – simply because the club swings back and down slightly *inside* the target line, stays quite *square* for a short time during impact, then of course, goes back *inside* the target line on the follow-through, as the body turns away. Many players believe the club should be swung backwards and forwards, on the target line, for as long as possible; but this is totally wrong, as the body has to turn both on the backswing and downswing. It should happen naturally.

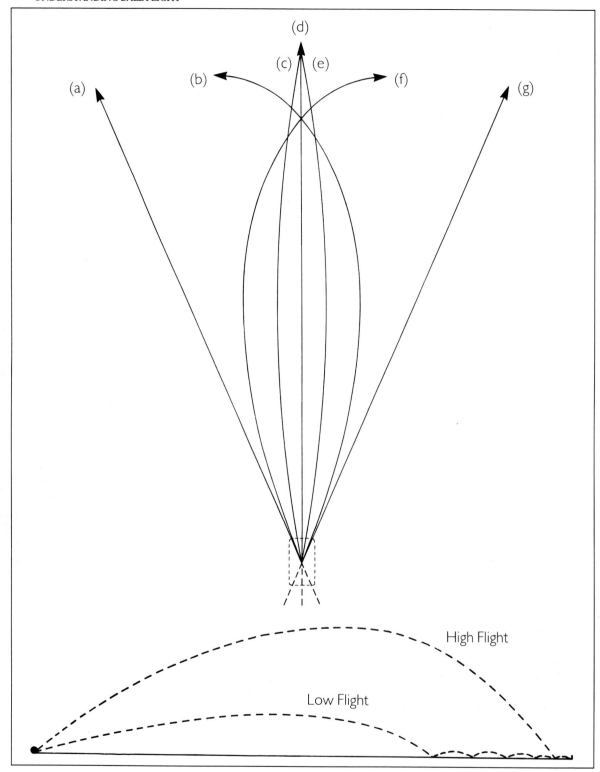

Slice

Over eighty-five per cent of golfers slice the ball, and of those, I estimate that half do not know why. Here are the reasons for that horrible little ball slicing. First of all, the ball has slice, or left to right sidespin (for right-handers), because the clubhead approaches the ball in an open-face position, and from an out-to-in direction. The clubhead has been allowed to stay *outside* or away from the target line on the downswing, and continues past the ball to the left or *inside* the target line. Because the clubface is not square to the target, the ball is struck a glancing blow which causes left to right spin. Sadly this is a very inefficient way to hit the ball and most of the energy is wasted, resulting in a curving flight and no distance. This shot is most golfers' enemy as it requires all the effort, yet produces no real reward.

Pull

The pull shot in golf is caused by the same swing as the slice but with the clubface in a closed position, causing the ball to start to the left of the target and continue on to the left. This is normally a strong shot and is often acceptable to the player, providing the ball does not finish too far off line. Slicers usually find that this pulled shot is the only way they can hit the ball a long way but are not sure when it is going to happen.

Hook

It is often said that golfers who hook the golf ball are, invariably, good players, and this is often quite true, provided they do not use a very poor hold on the club. The hook is normally caused by the clubhead approaching the ball from very much inside the target line with the face of the club in a closed or shut position then continuing past the ball outside the target line. This sort of swing, naturally, causes the ball to spin excessively from right to left with usually a low flight, causing the ball to run too much after landing. It does send the ball quite long distances, but it can rarely be controlled due to the excessive roll.

Fig 25 (left) Different flight trajectories, seen from above and from the side: (a) pull; (b) hook; (c) fade, landing on target; (d) straight; (e) draw, landing on target; (f) slice; (g) push. A high flight causes the ball to land softly with very little roll; a low trajectory causes the ball to roll forward considerably on landing.

Push

The same swing direction can also produce a push shot. This is the shot that simply starts to the right of the target and continues on more to the right. The difference is, in the push shot, the clubface is left open to the target, whereas in the hook the clubface is closed.

All these shots can be identified by watching the flight of the ball:

1.   If the ball starts to the left, and curves back (slices), the clubface was approaching the ball in an open position, from out-to-in.
2.   If the ball starts to the left, and continues to the left, again the clubface was approaching the ball from out-to-in but this time in a closed position.
3.   When the ball starts to the right, and curves back to the left (hooks), it follows that the clubface was closed when swinging very much from in-to-out.
4.   If the ball starts to the right and continues on to the right (push), the club face was delivered from in-to-out, but with the clubface open to the target.

10　Short Game Tips

Pitched or lofted half shots, often cause anxiety to even the good golfer. The feeling of having to 'baby' or 'coax' the ball is not one that comes easily. Hitting hard is fun and more natural.

These shots are mostly played with a pitching wedge or sand iron. The best way of playing them is to hold the club up to two inches further down the shaft, as this reduces the arc of the swing and the distance the club hits the ball. If the wedge usually hits the ball 90 yards, holding the club two inches down the shaft will hit it approximately 70 yards. The secret of all half shots is, however long your backswing, to accelerate the club past the ball. Even with a short swing, hit it firmly. Never decelerate – this causes legs and wrists to collapse with disastrous results to the shot. The follow-through should be as long as the backswing.

Short pitch shots are feared by many players and all sorts of wedges are manufactured to assist these players. I recommend a lofted pitching club as it is possible to hit the ball quite hard without sending it too far. Naturally the more loft you have, the higher you can hit the ball, without needing too much wrist action to get it airborne.

A slightly open stance is preferred for short pitches as this enables you to swing the club on a very slightly out to in arc. There should not be too much wrist action for these shots and the hold of the club should be firm but not tight. The main secret is to keep the arc constant. No jerks, no scoops but a brushing, sweeping action. Always hit past the ball towards the target.

The pendulum action is also preferred for these pitch shots. Swing the club back and forwards the same amount. Never use a long backswing and a short follow-through, or a short backswing and a long follow-through. These shots must be played with feel. Do not clutch the club too tightly as this will cause a pushing action. Swing the arms more than the wrists with the hands remaining passive. It is not necessary to move the weight very much on these shots but emphasis should be put on keeping the weight on the left side as the downswing starts. Too many players fall back at impact.

Fig 26   For the straightforward pitch shot with a lofted club (wedge or sand iron), the ball should be positioned midway between the feet. Once again, the knees should be slightly flexed, and a comfortable position should be adopted. The hands should be only slightly ahead of the ball, and the weight marginally favouring the left side. The clubface must be positioned so that there is lots of loft on it.

Fig 27   Note the fairly steep take-away, with the hands and arms doing most of the work. Because the feet are slightly open, the club does not go back on the inside plane, but follows the line of the feet.

Fig 28   This length of follow-through is all that is necessary. The clubface has remained open, and has been allowed to continue on towards the target.

Chip or run-up shots do not need a long swing and should only be played with the arms. A shallow arc is needed, as it is only necessary to roll the ball along the ground with anything between a 5- and a 9-iron. Most golfers prefer a 7-iron for this type of shot as it has an acceptable amount of loft and a manageable length of shaft. I recommend that this shot should be viewed in the same way as a long putt. The only difference is, it is played with a 7-iron and not a putter. A definite feel for the distance is essential and that feel comes largely from the hands, so do not hold the club tightly. A soft grip and gentle swing with the arms, will create the direction

Fig 29 Note how comfortable this position looks – knees slightly flexed, ball slightly back in the stance, and hands in front of the ball.

Fig 30 Front view of the backswing on the run-up shot. The arms are swinging the golf club back, with only a little wrist action. The body has barely moved.

Fig 31 The back view of the run-up shot. Again the arms are swinging the club head back on a slightly inside line. Note how low to the ground the clubhead is.

Fig 32 This is a good example of how the arms should swing the golf club past the ball, without any interference from the wrists. The knees and legs are still comfortably flexed, and the head and body are quite still.

Fig 33 Rear view of the follow-through – the clubhead travelling towards the target, with the arms doing most of the work.

and feel needed to play good run-up shots. The weight should be kept mainly on the left side through the swing. Always hit past the ball and on towards the target. This keeps the arc constant and smooth. It really is worth practising these shots as so many strokes can be saved by playing them properly.

When practising these important chip and pitch shots, do so with a friend or fellow competitor, as competition is the essence of all practice. It is important to try to simulate the pressure one experiences during a competition or important match. It is also important to learn how to play these shorter shots from difficult lies. Try them from down slopes, up slopes and side slopes. If you miss a green and have a chip or pitch to play, invariably you will have an awkward shot so don't just practise the straight-forward ones. You do not have the right to a good lie so learn to cope with every situation.

Practise with the clubface open, closed, with a punching action, and a smooth swinging action. Each type of swing will send the ball off at a different speed and trajectory. Have fun trying these very different positions. They are all important. Remember, any player who can improvise with these shots is a match for anyone.

11 Mastering Bunker Play

It always amazes amateurs when pros make bunker shots look easy; and pros find it difficult to understand why amateurs are so frightened of them.

Greenside Shot

If, for instance, you are faced with a greenside bunker shot – open the clubface slightly, use the normal grip but an inch or so further down the shaft, and open the stance slightly (left foot back for right handers). I do stress, open the club and stance *only slightly* as I see so many middle or high-handicap players who exaggerate these movements to extremes.

Always swing the club parallel to the feet for these shots as a slightly out-to-in action is required to extricate the ball. Because of this out-to-in swing, the club rises and descends a little more steeply than normal. The steeper swing imparts backspin, forcing the ball to rise quickly, and makes it stop on landing. This is the classic greenside bunker shot but there are other types of sand problems.

Having a mental picture of the entire operation is essential.

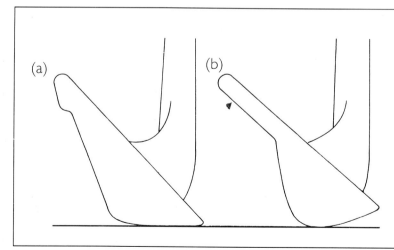

Fig 34 (a) The flat sole of the pitching wedge. The leading edge, being on the ground, cuts a divot and allows the player to loft the ball from poor lies; (b) shows the raised back edge of a good sand iron. This helps to bounce the club through the sand, making the follow-through much easier when in bunkers.

Fig 35 (left) The address for a normal bunker shot – ball positioned towards the left foot, clubface slightly open (lofted), and hands and weight slightly forward.

Fig 36 (right) Top of the backswing for the bunker shot – clubface open, arms swinging the club up without too much body movement.

Fig 37 (left) This is the position that all high-handicap golfers should aim for, when playing a bunker shot. The clubhead has been swung down and forward. The loft of the club has made the ball rise quickly.

Fig 38 (right) The completed follow-through for the bunker shot – the right knee has kicked forward, and the arms and club have continued on towards the target.

It is no use at all being frightened by sand. Imagine instead that the sand is soft grass. Playing from soft grass is exactly the same. You cannot put the club down immediately behind the ball because the club would disturb the grass and cause the ball to move. Next use the same open stance and upright swing as the shot from poor lies, but this time concentrate on taking a divot which starts one or two inches before impact and continues on two inches after. Many golfers call this a 'splash shot', as the club splashes into the sand (soft grass) and bounces off to produce a soft rising, controlled shot. For short bunker shots a large divot should be taken out, and for long bunker shots only a small, shallow divot is necessary. These normal bunker shots require lots of loft on the club so do not close the clubface or have the hands too far forward. Remember, loft is what is required, not just an open clubface. Opening the clubface does help to get the ball airborne, but it also sends the ball to the right. The action of creating loft on the club, or opening it, guarantees that the back edge of the sole of the club hits the sand at impact and causes the club to slide over the surface of the sand.

When the ball is not lying well, it is advisable to keep the clubface square so that it digs into the sand behind the ball and ejects them both together. Of course, it is not possible to hit the ball a long way in these circumstances, nor is it possible to impart backspin from a plugged lie. Nevertheless, it is important to create speed on approaching the ball, and to keep the clubface square and moving past the ball.

Long Shots

Long bunker shots are among the most difficult to play in golf. The bunker shot from around 60 to 80 yards is a particularly hard one as it is not quite a full shot with any club. I believe in using a sand iron for anything within range of this club because of the bounce on the sole. Other clubs have a relatively sharp leading edge which tends to cut into the sand. The sand wedge is more likely to bounce off the sand, which is exactly what is needed for this shot.

A three-quarter swing is most effective as the less movement introduced into the swing, the better. A steep, descending blow must be avoided. Instead, a sweeping arm action (no wrists) and good weight shift on the downswing should be used. Every effort to swing the club forwards should be encouraged. Never, ever try to scoop the ball out of a bunker. A constant arc with good balance is what is needed. On

51

finishing the swing, check to see if the hold on the club is as firm as it was during the swing – it should be!

Very Long Shots

The very long bunker shot can only be attempted if the face or lip of the bunker is not too high and if the ball is lying quite well. Really good players can risk a number 3 or 4 wood, from good lies in sand, as the sole of these clubs is perfect for bouncing. It is not advisable to use long irons from traps as the soles are too narrow and the loft is too little. A 4-iron is a possibility if the sand is firm and the lie is good but all the more lofted clubs are preferable.

A normal swing is necessary, but with the ball slightly back in the stance, perhaps one inch nearer the right foot than usual. Keep the backswing smooth and firm – never over-swing on this one. The most important thought must be to 'hit and move'. Swing the arms down to 'hit' the ball, and 'move' the weight forward on to the left side and out of the way. Once again do not stay back on the right foot in an effort to get the ball up. Move through the shot to hit the ball forward.

Down Slopes

When the ball is on a down slope in a bunker, play the shot from near the left foot with the stance and the face of the club open. Keep the weight on the left foot and, using a three-quarter swing, try to follow the slope with the downswing. This means that the weight should be on the left foot, particularly at impact, to enable the ball to be sliced out. I use the term 'sliced out' as this is exactly what happens if the stance and the face of the club are open enough.

Up Slopes

On uphill slopes, remember that the ball will fly higher automatically. This means a harder hit is necessary as a higher shot does not normally fly so far. It is not necessary to open the clubface or the stance for this type of shot, but do try to keep your body and the swing parallel to the slope. (Follow the line of the slope with the clubhead so the divot is not too deep.)

In this age of advanced technology it is possible to watch video tapes of your favourite players and to copy them playing these trouble shots. Very few players actually practise them and only go to the pro when things go wrong. That is why I recommend that you have a mental picture of the entire shot before even attempting to play it. Keep that picture in mind, follow the basic rules and sand will not present any more problems. Good professionals make these shots look easy.

12 Tackling Trouble Shots

Practising trouble shots should be fun. Just watch a good professional during a demonstration. He will always finish off with a few slices, hooks, low and high shots to entertain the crowd. Sadly, most amateurs think this is just amusement, but moving the ball in different directions and at different trajectories is a most important part of learning how to control it. Control is what golf is all about.

To play these trouble shots we do, of course, have to deviate from the basics. How much we deviate depends entirely on how much curve and flight we need to impart on the golf ball. For a fade, for example, we need to open our stance and the clubface slightly. For a slice, we need to open our stance and the clubface considerably more. Most golfers find the slice the easiest of the 'alternative' shots in golf. Remember though, when trying to slice purposely, the clubface position is just as important as the stance and body position – it must be open in relation to them.

My own recommendation is always to aim the clubface at the target, and alter the stance and body alignment as much as is necessary to deviate from the straight shot. Swing the club along the line of the feet, both up and down. The reason I think the clubface should be on line with the target is that the stance determines how much the club is swung across the target line; but if the clubface is square to the target, it ensures that the ball 'returns' there. After all, whether we fade, slice or hook intentionally we always require the ball to finish near the target. I have never found anyone who argues with this fact.

The set-up for the *draw* or hook is naturally the opposite to that of the fade or slice. Once more the set-up starts with aiming the clubface. Square the face to the target, draw the right foot and right side back as much as the shot requires and swing the club along the line of the feet. This is called an 'in-to-out' swing, because the club is being swung inside the target line on the backswing and outside it on the follow-through. As the clubface is square to the target, the ball starts to the right of the line and curves back towards it, once again finishing on the target. Simply closing the clubface is not enough, it just sends the ball to the left.

Fig 39 (right) Geoff Hawkes. The famous backhanded shot in the 1987 Epson Grand Prix at St Pierre where, instead of facing the hole, he turned his back to the flag, turned the toe of the club inside, and played the shot one handed.

Fig 41 (left) A steep backswing is essential when the ball is in long grass. The steeper the approach to the ball, the less the grass affects the golf-club.

Fig 42 (right) Just after impact in long grass. The outside-in downswing has been effected with the clubface still held open. The club has been accelerated down and through – this is essential.

The *low straight shot* is quite easy as the adjustment or deviation from normal is quite small. Simply, move the feet in front of the ball or move the ball back towards the right foot (left for left-handers) and swing normally. Moving the ball back in the stance keeps the hands ahead of the ball and delivers the clubhead in a less lofted position. This causes the ball to fly lower than normal.

As one would expect, the *high shot* also needs very little deviation. Whereas the low shot requires the ball to be moved back in the stance, the higher shot requires the ball to be moved forward, or towards the left foot for the right-hander. As the ball is moved forward the hands stay behind the ball, creating loft on the clubface. This loft is necessary to send the ball on a higher trajectory. Opening the clubface by itself is not enough, it just sends the ball off to the right.

The essential considerations for the slice and hook are to swing the club along the line of the open stance for the slice, and along the line of the closed stance for the hook. It does not matter how open or closed the clubface appears to the player after altering the stance and body position. Get the angles right. If the rules are followed any player can change the shape of his game. Have fun trying these experiments, but

Fig 40 (left) Seve Ballesteros – possibly the greatest trouble-shot player ever. He not only has a great imagination for these shots, but he also never attempts anything unless he is convinced that he can do it.

Fig 43 (left) This shows the ball played from well back in the stance. Note how the hands are in front of the ball, causing it to look delofted. This obviously makes the ball fly much lower.

Fig 44 (right) The ball is well forward, towards the left foot. The hands are visibly behind the ball, creating loft on the clubface. From this address position the ball will fly much higher.

get a friend or even your golf pro to check that you really are making these adjustments. Most players do move the feet, but close or open the face of the club as they change their aim. The procedure remains the same. Aim the clubface, take a grip, position the stance, then position the body – *Club, Grip, Stance, Posture.*

13 Good News about Bad Lies

Hitting the ball from bad lies and heavy grass needs the same action as used in the bunker shot. Whether in long grass or a poor lie, open the stance a little, left foot behind the line (for right handers), swing the arms up a little more than usual, and concentrate on hitting the bottom of the ball as the weight moves forward. The open stance causes the club to be swung up fairly sharply and downwards in a steeper arc than normal, slightly across the target line. This action causes the ball to rise quickly and escape from the poor lie or long grass.

Playing from sloping lies should be considered quite normal by every golfer, because very few golf courses are perfectly flat. Nevertheless, some of these situations do cause problems for different types of player.

Above or Below the Feet

Any player who slices the ball, prefers to have the *ball above the level of the feet* as this makes the player swing on a flatter plane and compensates for the slice; but the reverse is the case for the player who hooks. Swinging flatter, for the golfer who hooks, only accentuates the hook. The cure is very simple, as we know the ball will curve to the left if our feet are 'below' the ball. Just aim slightly to the right, with the ball a little nearer the right foot than normal. Shortening the hold on the club will give the control necessary in this awkward situation, and make sure that the wrists do not become too active as this also will tend to close the clubface.

When the ball genuinely is *below the feet* this presents the reverse and more difficult problem. This causes the player to swing higher and more out-to-in, causing the ball to slice with very little power. To counteract this, keep the weight more on the heels, flex the knees more than usual, and hold the club at full length. During the swing, keep the weight on the heels and keep the hands and arms more flexible to eliminate any movement which may cause the weight to fall forward.

Fig 45 Leaning back slightly, to allow me to swing the clubhead parallel to the up-slope. Note how the right shoulder has dropped a little, and the knees are slightly flexed.

Fig 46   The wrong way to address the ball for an uphill lie. The weight and hands are too far forward, which will cause the club to approach the ball at a steep angle, and a deep divot will be the result.

Fig 47   A good example of the weight settling on the left side, which will allow me to swing the club down the slope rather than trying to scoop it up.

Uphill and Downhill Lies

Uphill lies do not present too many problems to us as the ball invariably rises quickly from this sort of situation. Posture, however, is important as the back or spine should be at right angles to the uphill slope. Feel how your weight rests on the right foot and counteract this by leaning forward, avoiding altering the back angle in relation to the ground. This means bending the right leg slightly. Use a less lofted club, as the ball will fly higher automatically, and make an effort to follow the slope with the clubhead. Play the ball from the middle of the stance, and allow for the slight hook that should occur.

The *downhill lie* is considered the most difficult of all, as it is so hard to get the clubhead into the back of the ball. The set-up at address is particularly important. Again, the angle of the spine must be set at 90° to the ground, this time with the 'feeling' of leaning forward maintained and the left knee slightly bent. This enables you to swing the club 'up and down the slope'. The ball will fly with a lower trajectory, so use a slightly more lofted club. It is not possible to get backspin on this shot.

If a long iron or wood is needed from a downhill lie, play the ball from nearer the left foot and aim left as the ball will almost certainly slice. Balance is the key to these awkward stances, so do not use too much body action. A controlled hand and arm action always gives the best results.

Hazards and Strategy

When dealing with a poor lie – whether in a bunker, in heavy grass or even amongst trees – remember always that two major things are involved: trajectory and distance. Only the very best players seem to combine the two elements which make them look great to the ordinary player.

Elevation is normally a prerequisite, simply to extricate the ball. The next consideration must be to send the ball the correct distance. It is often easy to get out of a bunker, but this is not enough if the next shot is still impossible.

The same is true when playing from trees. Playing the ball to a safe piece of ground is worthless if the trees block out the next shot. One golden rule is to use a less lofted club for chipping out of trees, even a 3- or 4-iron if the intervening branches are low. I have played in so many pro-ams when my partners have used a 9-iron, or so, from under trees only to find the ball climbing into the branches and returning to its original position. It is possible to hit the ball over 100 yards from under trees using a half swing with a 3-iron, so consider this rather than trying to squeeze a 9-iron through a small gap in the branches.

This ploy is also advisable when faced with a difficult shot where the ball has to be run up a steep bank. Do not use a lofted club to try to land on the crest of the hill. Play the shot with a 3- or 4-iron. The bounces are much more regular with a less lofted club. Gary Player is a real star at this shot. Play it just like a long putt, with very little wrist action, and the ball will tumble up the slope with a good deal of control.

One of the most difficult shots, is when the ball has just run off the edge of the green and come to rest a foot or so in the thicker grass. For most amateur players this is a problem, as the normal pitch can flop a few inches or scuttle right across the green. Try the shot the real experts play, which uses the sand iron, and attempt to hit the middle of the ball with the leading edge, or the sole of the club. This in effect means a deliberate, topped shot. As soon as the leading edge makes contact with the middle of the ball it shoots out quickly, guaranteeing to make the ball run out of the grass and on to the green. With only a little practice anyone can be effective with this unusual shot.

Thick grass is always a problem for the golfer, but do remember that long grass does wrap around the club, so these shots must be played with the clubface open. They are like a normal bunker shot as a steep swing is necessary. Plenty of loft on the club, and lots of authority on the downswing is what is called for. Select the loft and distance needed before starting the swing, then play the shot positively, keeping your head still and the clubhead travelling down and through.

Playing a safety shot is not always a negative way to play golf. It is frequently the positive way to play a particular hole. For instance, if you cannot quite reach a particular green with a long shot, it is often a good idea to play well short. This gives you an opportunity to play a lofted pitch shot, with a good degree of spin, rather than playing a particularly difficult run-up shot around a bunker or over a steep mound. You will often see top professionals taking irons off tees, even though a good drive may get within 20 or 30 yards of the green. These players know that a lofted wedge or sand iron from around 70 or 80 yards is more reliable than a tricky 30 yards run-up shot to a tough pin position.

Finally, find a slope on your practice ground and have fun trying each of these awkward lies. You will be amazed at how good you become after a few practice shots.

Fig 48 The wrong way to address a downhill shot. From this set-up, the golf club will collide with the ground far too soon.

14 Confident Putting

It has been said that putting is a game of its own. The reason for this is that although it needs a reliable action, confidence plays a more important part in this golf shot. Putting is a part of the game that constantly baffles us. It is such a fine art that constant tuning is the order of the day, almost every day.

There are many, many ways of putting, and every golfer has his or her own theories on this game within a game. Many top players, like Bernhard Langer and Lee Trevino, carry up to ten putters to each tournament and often these putters are the same brand but with different lofts, lies and shaft lengths. This is done to cope with the different feel one has each day.

Arnold Palmer was one of the greatest putters of all time at the height of his career. His secrets were a solid attacking action, bundles of confidence, and a bundle of putters in the back of his car. Arnold loved to change the grips, lofts and weights of his favourite putters. Very few world-class players stick to one putter – that is a thing of the past. With tournaments in all parts of the world these great players realise that certain putters perform better on certain types of green.

Few touring players use the old type of blade putter now. Most use a centre shaft, offset type, as they are more forgiving. This means that the centre spot, or sweet spot, on this type of club is wider, and the ball rolls smoothly even when not hit absolutely in the middle of the club.

A number of top-class players adopt a reverse overlap grip on the putter. This means that all the fingers of the right hand fit on the handle, and the index finger of the left hand fits over the fingers of the right hand.

Bernhard Langer really set a fashion a few years ago when he reorganised his putting. He spent some months learning to putt with his left hand below his right. He believes that this grip helps him to pull the clubhead past the ball on the line of the target. The normal putting grip simply did not work for him. Since the change Bernhard has become one of the best putters in the world. It took a great deal of patience and practice, but it was worth the enormous change.

Fig 49   The way I address the ball for putting. This will not work for everyone, as putting is such an individual part of the game. Comfort and direction are essential.

Fig 50   Note that the putter has been taken back at a fairly low angle, with the arms swinging freely. Invariably, wristy putters are inconsistent.

Fig 51   Again, the arms have accelerated the putter forward on a low arc, and in the direction of the hole. Smoothness and feel are essential for consistent putting.

Grain

Any golfer who has played in very warm countries knows what grain is. Some greens in the UK also have grain but not for the same reason. Grain, or nap as it is known, is when the grass grows in a certain direction, not straight up. It looks as if the grass has been grown a little long and has been flattened. In warm countries the grass grows towards the nearest large expanse of water, or towards the hot sun (usually south). This flattened grass has a great effect on the rolling golf ball. When the grass grows from north to south and the putt is also from north to south the ball rolls much further than normal. If your putt is from south to north, against the grain, the putt will be slower than normal. Naturally when putting across the grain, east to west, the ball will always curve towards the south, or along the grain.

The easy way to learn where the grain is running is to stand on each side of the line of the putt to see which way the grass looks shiny, and which way it looks dark. When it looks shiny the putt is fast, and when it looks dark the putt is slow. Practice is the only way to learn effectively, but don't be frightened to ask experienced players if you are looking for the correct signs on the green.

In the UK some greens appear to have grain, but this is mainly caused by incorrect mowing. If the greenkeeper mows the same way each time, the grass gets flattened in one direction. This also causes the ball to follow the grain instead of running straight on a flat green. Again, looking for the shine will help decide whether the putt is fast or slow.

Direction and Distance

The plain facts are, there are only two elements to putting. One is the distance factor, the other is the direction. Most of us are good at one or other of these, but few of us do both successfully or consistently.

To obtain feel, the hold of the putter must be light, as tight muscles have no feel or touch. The hands must fit perfectly and must not oppose each other. To control direction, the putter should be drawn back smoothly, on a slightly inside or slightly curving arc, without too much wrist action (which would alter the angle of the putter face during the swing). Again a pendulum-type action is preferable, and a definite strike or acceleration is needed on the downswing to make the ball roll smoothly along the green. The length of the follow-through should be roughly the same as the backswing. Never stop at impact. Swing the club past the ball and try to finish with it on line with the hole.

Many golfers lift the putter up as they hit the ball in an effort to impart top spin. This is completely unnecessary. The putter should only come off the ground slightly on the backswing, and the same amount on the follow through.

Short putts are missed either through carelessness or because they are not hit firmly enough. The area of the green near the hole is the most used and most trodden part – eventually, everyone finishes up near the hole! This means that the grass here is uneven and often bumpy. Every golfer knows that when the ball rolls near the hole it tends to bobble or wander off. In my opinion, this is why the best short putters are players like Nick Faldo and Greg Norman, because they hit the ball into the hole firmly. Short putts must be dealt with firmly and positively.

Long putts require more feel than short ones, because speed or judgement of distance is essential. Few long putts are unsuccessful due to the incorrect line, but many are unsuccessful because they do not travel the correct distance. The only way to judge the correct distance is to hold the putter loosely. A long swinging action is far more effective than a short sharp stroke. Feel comes with a smooth flowing action and is essential to consistency. The arc the putter swings on must also be consistent, so the arms and the putter angle should not change. The best practice exercise is to throw six balls on to the green, then try to hit them all the same distance. You will be amazed at the results.

Nearly all good putters, like Ben Crenshaw, swing their arms freely and smoothly. They give themselves plenty of room and concentrate on feel and timing. My own opinion is that good putters, like great players, are able to compose themselves under pressure. They never panic or allow themselves to be hurried. They have a regular routine and never vary it. Poor putters try every theory they hear or read about, and change putters constantly. Putting is always about practice, consistency and above all patience.

15 Swing Faults and their Cures

Slice

The great majority who slice, or even tend to slice, should first check their hold on the club. Invariably, their hands will be too far on top, or on the left side of the handle. This also causes the shoulders to aim to the left, so make quite certain that the following checks are strictly adhered to.

First, aim the clubhead properly and squarely at the target. Take this book to the practice ground, or ask someone to read these instructions to you while you do the actions.

Next, hold the club with both hands on the top of, or better still to the right of, the handle. When that is achieved, *without disturbing the clubhead position*, make certain your right shoulder is tucked back behind as if you are already starting to turn on the backswing. This is called 'closing the shoulders'. If this is done enough, the club almost certainly will be drawn back on an inside path during the backswing. Slicers rarely turn their shoulders enough during the backswing, so make a definite effort to turn the right side of the body right out of the way. On arrival, at the top of the backswing, check that the club shaft is aiming at your target. If it is aiming to the left of your target – turn more until it is at least on line or even to the right of it.

The next movement is the crucial one. Do *not* turn the shoulders back towards the ball until the arms have started their downward movement. This means, try to square the clubhead *before* your weight moves too far to the left.

Slicers invariably swing their bodies ahead of the golf club on the downswing, causing a late hit and a marvellous spinning slice. Just allow the weight to move forward by easing the legs and hips back to their original position. A well known saying among professionals and leading amateurs is, 'Bad players swing themselves, and good players swing the golf club.' In other words, do not shove your upper body in the way of the golf club, particularly during the downswing. Simply swing the club down to the waiting ball in the space

Fig 52   This action is one that I do not recommend to any of my pupils. The body and arms have raced ahead of the clubface, leaving it wide open. This is suicide for the long-handicap player.

created by the turning of the right side. This is, of course, the inside line.

Slicers would be well advised to hit early on the downswing, rather than late. Remember, late is exactly that – too late. Striking early means you have more time. Time and room are the two most valuable things in the golf swing. Turning the right side creates room for the club on the backswing and downswing. Turning the left side creates the room and direction for the follow-through. In the middle of these two turns the arms swing the club up to the top of the swing, down to meet the ball, and up again for the follow-through.

Hook

Golfers who hook the ball, do so because their clubface is closed on approaching the ball from inside the target line direction. These players should first check their hold of the club. First, aim the bottom edge of the clubface at the intended target. Next, put both hands on the handle so that the left hand is mainly on the left side of the handle, and the right hand on the top. This kind of hold tends to open the clubhead during the swing – just the thing for hookers.

To avoid hooking, swing the club and your arms up more than usual on the backswing, and shift the weight over to the left side a little earlier on the downswing. This action creates a slightly later hit on the downswing, causing the clubface to stay open longer and eliminating the hook.

One thing to remember is, if you have been hooking the ball you have probably been aiming it to the right of the target. After changing the hold on the club, the ball will no longer hook. Instead, the ball probably will fly to the right of where you think you are aiming. Now you need to readjust your stance. Any friend can check this aim for you, or you can simply put a club along the line of your toes to see where you are aiming.

Whether trying to cure a slice or hook, it is always worth laying a club down parallel to your feet to check your aim. The way you address the ball determines the way you will swing the club, so check that aim carefully – not just the line of the feet, but the shoulder line too.

A hooker must learn to swing the club more like a slicer, to eliminate his problem; and a slicer must learn the hooker's habit, to cure his.

Really good players can change their actions to spin the ball

Fig 53   This is more like it. The arms and hands are level with the ball as the clubface makes contact. Note, too, that my eyes are still slightly behind the ball.

Fig 54   This is the set-up which should be used for a draw or slight hook. Note the right foot has been drawn back slightly, as has the right shoulder. This encourages the golf club to be swung on the inside path.

Fig 55   The front view of setting-up for a draw or slight hook. As the right shoulder is drawn back, it follows that the ball should be moved further back in the stance.

Fig 56   The club is driving past the ball after impact, in the direction of the target. Note how, half-way through, it is already pointing in the right direction.

either way at will, but most high-handicap players find changing their habits desperately difficult. Good golf is not just in the mind, it requires good basic training and, needless to say, practice. Practising really can be fun, and should be encouraged. The fun part comes from working at a certain thing, and being successful. It is impossible to be successful quickly without practising.

Topping and Fluffing

Topping and fluffing are often caused by the same fault. Instead of the bottom of the swing being immediately underneath the ball, it is either too far forward or behind. Naturally, this means the weight has shifted from its original position, and not returned to it at impact. The only other way to top the ball, is to allow the left arm to collapse at impact. As both arms are fairly straight at the address position, they should return to being straight at impact. A few trial swings, in slow motion, will help the player to get the feel of this straightening action. Curl or fold the right arm on the backswing, then make a conscious effort to straighten it on the downswing and follow-through.

The most common fault which causes these inconsistencies in the hitting area is shoulder tilt. Sadly, many golfers believe that the left shoulder dictates the backswing and must be pushed under the chin to obtain the correct turn. This is definitely the wrong way to go about turning. Prove this by turning your back to the sun so that it casts a shadow in front of you, and make a practice swing, trying to move the left shoulder under the chin while watching the shadow of your head. You will notice that your head will dip on the backswing, and lift on the downswing.

This inconsistency in the head movement is enough to cause topping or fluffing. The cure is quite simple. Turn with your back to the sun, again, but this time just turn the right shoulder behind your head, or 'out of the way' as we call it, then swing down naturally. This time the shadow of your head will hardly move at all. I say 'hardly' move as everyone's head moves a little, even the great players.

Never try to force the left shoulder under the chin on the backswing and never force the right shoulder under the chin on the downswing. If the shoulders turn properly, or flat, the head stays in a high but constant position, only moving as the right side and shoulder clears forward, towards the target on the follow-through.

Also, never worry about the 'head-up', as so many amateur golfers call it. Try, instead, to find what causes it so it does not happen. Concentrate the eyes on the back of the ball, where the clubhead should strike, rather than glue the head down during the swing, which causes too much tension in the arms, neck and shoulders, and so stops the shoulders from turning properly. Don't be frightened of checking the backswing. One of Jack Nicklaus's favourite thoughts is turning the shoulders fully. If he is so keen on it we should realise that it is important to everyone who plays golf. Making the correct turn on the backswing gives us all the chance of delivering the club to the ball correctly and efficiently.

As most of golf's problems start on the backswing, make every effort to check each stage. Ask a friend to check to see if the shaft is actually aiming at your target at the top of the backswing. I am a great believer in practising with a friend. It is much more fun and much more beneficial. We cannot see ourselves swing, we can only be guided by our own feelings. Others can give us the real truth, if they know what to look for.

I also believe that video cameras can help us identify obvious faults like overswinging, swinging too upright, swinging too flat, and bad foot and leg movements. If you are not happy with your results on the course, ask your pro to set the camera up for you in the most important positions. (Few amateurs take the pictures from the correct angles.) This is a certain way to find out how you really swing. Do not listen to people who constantly tell you what you are doing wrong, though. What you really want to know, is what to do to cure the fault. This is positive, and the only advice you need. Remember, you can chart your progress by watching the flight of the ball. The ball is still the best teacher if you can read it. Know your spin and know your golf.

Shanking

Every amateur wants to know how to cure shanking, or socketing as some call it. I suppose that because poor players swing their bodies more than the golf club, they are more prone to hitting the ball near the heel. Hitting the ball on the shank, is only a little worse than hitting it with just the heel.

Quite simply, the shank is caused because the club is swung down on the outside arc on approaching the ball. There can be many reasons for this. One is starting the downswing with the right shoulder leading the way. Another is hitting too late, leaving the clubface far too open. Some people even move their head forward, causing them to topple towards the ball.

As mentioned earlier, the cure is really all we need to know. As the arms swing up on the backswing, turn the shoulders. Leave them turned as the club is swung down, with an early rather than late hit. This will help to square the clubhead before impact and keep the club on the inside line. Do not swing from in-to-out but down on the inside. Strike the ball, then swing forward and slightly to the left of the target. This action encourages the clubhead to close, and keeps the heel away from the ball.

One sure way of practising the correct swing and obtaining the correct mental picture is to place several balls, side by side, about three or four inches apart. Hit the first one with a chipping action, then address the next and hit it with a pitching action. Hit the next with a three-quarter swing, then lastly on to the full swing. This exercise helps to get the picture of hitting the ball towards the toe of the club rather than allowing you to swing the clubhead down on the outside arc. When swinging the club back and forward, feel the arms

Fig 57   (left) This is the usual cause when players shank. The shoulders have turned to the left too early, and the club has been allowed to come down outside the line of the ball.

Fig 58   (right) This is the correct downswing. The shoulders and hips are still square to the line – therefore the clubhead has been encouraged to swing down on the inside path.

swinging or brushing the right hip and side. It is only when the right arm moves away from the body that the socket or shank appears.

Practise this action in slow motion until you get the picture and feel in your mind. Never hurry an experiment. Watch the clubhead as it approaches the ball and passes it. Feel it closing and continuing on past. Speed is not essential when trying something new; knowledge and feel are. You will not be frightened of this shot, any more, if you know why it happens.

16   Tournament Play

In my view there are two types of competitors in golf as well as all other sports. There are those who look good, the really stylish well balanced players; and there are the real workers, or battlers, like Lee Trevino or Gary Player. They don't have the balance or flow of a Ballesteros, or a Faldo, but they make up for this deficiency by having what is commonly known as 'bottle' or courage. Every twenty or thirty years someone like Jack Nicklaus comes along who has all these qualities, and proves it by rewriting the record books.

Most golf professionals believe that it is easier to teach a pupil a good golf swing, than to teach a pupil to *compete* at a very high level. It is impossible to know exactly what a player is thinking when he or she is under pressure, although it is possible to 'psych' a competitor up before an important event. The Americans and Russians have been working on this for many years, in other sports. More and more books and cassette tapes are becoming available every year which help the golfer to concentrate solely on the job in hand.

Most long-handicap golfers do not have the ability to think properly in pressure situations, because they are not used to competing often enough. When they play friendly matches at weekends there is no real pressure, so when they are on their own in a different situation, they often are frightened of letting themselves down and they worry too much.

The correct way to face any stressful situation is to relax, and assess it carefully. If the brain is occupied in assessing the situation properly it does not have the time to fear anything. If a player has done his homework – like learning distances on a particular course, and learning how far they can hit each club – the only thing left to concentrate on, is making a good swing. Knowing his own consistent 'shape' and 'flight' is something that every player should recognise. Seasoned players do these things automatically and very quickly, but the long-handicap golfer must think more and take a little longer to sort these things out.

Any high-handicap golfer can plan a round of golf. For instance, if the player knows roughly how far he hits the ball and what his strengths and weaknesses are, there should not

Fig 59   (right) Jack Nicklaus in a typical pose. His concentration is awesome.

be a problem playing to his handicap. Disasters only occur when silly chances are taken.

Preparation is, of course, essential to performing well in a big event. A few practice shots prior to playing are invaluable. It is impossible to guarantee a decent score on the first few holes, unless a player has done at least some homework. Even a few chips and putts can establish a feel for the day. A good professional would not dream of starting a tournament without a good practice session. I think that a player who does not practice before an important match is extremely 'brave' indeed. Sensible players arrive at the club at least ten minutes early and hit a few balls, even if only in a net. This helps the muscles to tone up, and will certainly help one's confidence on the first tee.

Top players do not leave these things to chance. They do their homework before a tournament, so that they play confidently when the event starts. Competing in an important event is all about being in control. If you can control your mind, you can control your actions. This in turn controls the golf ball.

There are very few natural golfers. The golf swing is a fairly complicated thing and needs total concentration. After all, there are all sorts of different shots to be dealt with in every round. No two golf courses are the same – they all demand a different plan, and different thinking.

Jack Nicklaus believes that the player with the largest armoury wins the largest number of tournaments. However, golf is not just played with golf clubs, but also with the golfing brain. Each shot and each situation needs assessing properly, and this action takes practice, just as the golf swing does. In match play, you must consider what your opponent is doing. Rely on your favourite shot, or club, to give yourself encouragement; or confuse your opponent. Tactics play an enormous part in match-play golf. Medal play is literally a game of patience. One poor hole at the start of a round is not a disaster. Even when playing well, there are always one or two holes that can be improved. It is the player who does not show any emotion in difficult situations who usually comes out on top.

Whenever I play exhibitions, or pro-ams, I am usually told about a new young star at the particular club, and have often been asked to have a look at him or her. Invariably though, the members have said that although the young person is a good player and hits the ball well, the junior 'does not have the temperament for big time golf'.

This, in my view, is very unfair of the adult members,

Fig 60 (right) Tommy Horton playing out of a bunker, before going on to win the 1978 Dunlop Masters.

because each great player I meet has a different temperament. They can't all be wrong, or right. The only things they have in common are the desire to do well, and the ability to concentrate for those few vital seconds when they have been under extreme pressure. They all cope in a different way. How do we know if so and so has the wrong temperament until they are put under extreme pressure.

I believe we should encourage our younger players and improve their technique. They, and they alone, eventually will find out if they have the 'bottle' to react positively when they reach those really important situations.

Concentrating on the job in hand and assessing the situation intelligently can save as many shots on the course as three hours of practice on the driving range. Every good pro I know could save a middle-handicap player two or three shots per round, without improving his golf swing.

I have recently heard from the medical profession and from Alan Fine, Britain's leading sports psychologist, that great strides are being made in the psychological aspects of top competitors in all sports. The medical men are of course the professionals in this field and I am extremely interested in their views. After all, we are all looking for permanent cures not, as I have said many times before, odd gimmicks.

Preparing ourselves for important events is a very necessary part of competing successfully. Achieving a positive but relaxed mental state before actually playing must be the ideal way to perform at one's best, as I explain in Chapter 18. But positive thinking on its own is not enough. The golf ball has no brain and no confidence, it only reacts to the clubhead being wielded by the player. Neither Timothy Gallwey, in America, nor Alan Fine could play golf with awful golf swings, even though they might be supremely confident. The player must learn about himself both mentally and technically. Of course, a good mental attitude combined with a good golf swing is the ultimate aim. Jack Nicklaus has probably been as near perfection as any player over the past twenty years. Most of this was achieved through intense training.

The plain facts are that we cannot cater for the bad bounces, everybody gets them. What we can do is to train ourselves to accept them, and also train ourselves to play the ball from any bad lie or difficult situation. The player with the complete range of shots can cope with any situation. American golfers are extremely good at this – they are trained, as young men, in their sporting universities. I wish we had the same facilities in the UK.

So many amateurs follow one bad shot with another,

simply because they rush on without any thought, just panic. Naturally this leads to further problems. Each shot is different and requires a different swing. Women are particularly vulnerable here as they feel they do not want to hold up other players. Panic sets in and they need to hit the ball far more often because of this. More shots take more time and so on. The easy route is often the best. Long-handicap players are not expected to make marvellous recoveries or spectacular shots.

There is no substitute for experience and playing with better players than oneself is the fastest way to learn. Good players seem to assess situations faster, mainly because they are starting their assessment while approaching the ball. Half the important decisions are made before the good player reaches the ball. Things to consider include wind direction, firmness of the ground, slope of the terrain both at the ball and near the green, and whether it is you or your opponent to play first. The only decisions left to make are first what club is needed and then how to swing for that particular shot.

Don't hurry any decision and don't play any shot without being confident that your decision is correct. Plan ahead and do start your planning before you approach the ball.

17 Fitness and Golf

Fortunately the average player does not have to be supremely fit, as golf is not a particularly physical sport. It is necessary, however, to be supple and to have enough stamina to concentrate and swing the golf club efficiently, for at least four hours. However, most good players are quite fit, and play consistently because they have strong legs and an active brain.

My own opinion is, that actually practising golf itself is sufficient for the average person. One useful exercise though, is to add lots of weight to an old wooden club and to swing it regularly. Whereas a normal wood probably weighs about fourteen ounces, a good efficient practice club should weigh nearer twenty ounces.

Use the heavy club exactly as you would use a normal one. The correct swing will help strengthen first the hands, then arms, shoulders, back and legs. The above sequence is, in my view, in the correct order. Strong hands are extremely important to control the golf club during the swing – most importantly at the start of the downswing and, of course, at impact. The arms support the hands and the club, and keep the arc constant. The shoulders need to turn and make room for the arms and hands, and the back and legs have to support the rest of the body. Frequent practice with the heavy club helps to exercise all these parts of the body, which are needed so much because they are the main parts used when we normally swing the club.

Always start the above exercise by using half swings, then gradually build up each session to full, driver type swings. This is an excellent exercise for building up the correct muscles for the game.

Naturally legs are important to golf as players are using their feet and legs for long periods, especially during competitions. The occasional jog (not too far at first) is a marvellous way to keep the legs and lungs in good shape. Jogging is far more enjoyable if done with a friend, as it can be boring on one's own. Remember to use good jogging shoes, because the wrong shoes can cause serious damage to the feet.

Exercise depends entirely on the age of the golfer. The young player, with ideas of turning professional, should be

Fig 61   (right) Gary Player – who exercised more than any other golfer during his younger days, and still exercises even though he is in his mid-fifties. Gary believes that a fit body enables the brain to think more clearly.

very careful about any type of exercise and is advised to go to a proper physical training expert to work out a schedule. Middle-aged or older golfers should only exercise gently, but fairly frequently, to keep their muscles supple. The weighted club is a 'must' for this type of player and can be used twice a day to obtain maximum benefit. Holding and swinging two clubs together is a good compromise if no weighted club is readily available. This has the same effect, and makes one club feel light and manageable after the exercise.

Deep breathing exercises each morning are an easy way of keeping the lungs functioning properly. Always start this exercise by blowing all the stale air out first. Then take really deep breaths for about thirty seconds. The best place for breathing exercises is at an open window or outside, certainly not during the evening at your local pub!

Hitting balls from rough grass or poor lies is a very good way to keep fit for those unused to strenuous exercise. Simply throw a few balls into the rough and try to hit them properly to a given target. This exercise is a great way to learn how to control the club and the ball.

It is very fashionable, for women particularly, to attend aerobic classes. This form of exercise is recommended highly, and should be entertaining for men also! Aerobic exercises use all the muscles needed in golf, and are far more fun than pushing weights about at the local gymnasium.

I truly believe that a fit body enables the mind and the body to function with real confidence. Gary Player always felt that the fitter he was, the better and more confidently he played. He certainly is fit, and is still playing marvellous golf on the American senior circuit, even though he is approaching his mid-fifties.

18 Mental Attitude

A great deal is being talked about the mental aspect of golf, as great strides are being made in other sports. Several golf psychologists have emerged in recent years with some success. These positive thinking gurus are teaching golfers to believe in themselves and not to allow bad or negative thoughts to enter their minds when the pressure builds up. In my experience, positive thinking is thinking only of the job in hand, and concentrating entirely on how to go about carrying out that job.

One clever and positive way is, when faced with a particularly difficult or important shot, to cast your mind back to the time you played a perfect shot in similar circumstances. Picture that occasion in your mind, and visualise the ball floating through a clear blue sky and landing safely on the green or fairway. Remember, too, how you went about preparing that great shot, and follow that same pattern again. Playing good golf is the result of constant repetition. While the mind is occupied with these positive thoughts, you don't have time to be nervous or pessimistic!

When approaching the first tee, after hitting a few practice shots of course, take a few evenly spaced deep breaths and walk at an even pace. Rushing up to a tee in a panic invariably spells disaster. On approaching the first shot of the day convince yourself that you have made the right choice of club. Plan exactly what sort of shot you are going to hit and exactly how you are going to swing. Once the game has started trust your golf swing and keep the same rhythm for each shot, whatever the situation. Consistent rhythm leads to consistent shots. Consistency breeds confidence, and confidence wins matches.

The best swingers do not always win events – it is the clever player who wins. The player who sticks to his game plan and is in full control of himself is a hard man to beat. My old coach, Max Faulkner, used to say, 'Don't give your opponent the advantage of seeing you upset'. Smile when things do not go according to plan, and your opponent will be puzzled. Golf is a very unpredictable game and the bad bounces must be taken with the good.

I play in many pro-ams with amateurs who expect to play their best each time. Some get very upset if they start poorly – and my job is mainly one of encouragement, with the odd tip thrown in to help their game. This must be done quite calmly, as some players get very depressed when they have paid large sums to play in these competitions.

It is a great joy to play with the amateur who laughs and tries hard. Fourballs, foursomes and pro-ams are team games, and each team member should encourage the other. I believe it is possible to change one's character – certainly on the golf course, as you're playing a game anyway. All games should be fun, but should also be played with winning in mind.

Women golfers are not often great competitors unless they reach very low handicaps. Most long-handicap women love to chat on the way round, and generally enjoy the walk or the game. Many people think that this is the only way to play golf, but this is not the way to improve one's game. My own favourite game with women players is hugs for pars and kisses for birdies. This is a real fun game, and very competitive!

The real problems on the golf course are often water hazards, or out of bounds fences. The only way to deal with such hazards is to fix your mind totally on the opposite side of the fairway or green. Concentrate on aiming the clubface and the stance on the safe side, and concentrate the mind entirely on the target in the distance. In your mind visualise the ball flying directly at the safe area.

Three putting is a real shaker to all golfers. Professionals talk about putting far more than amateurs because their living depends on whether the ball drops in or stays out. I do find that high-handicap players actually enjoy putting, as it is the rest of their game that can be improved most. For those who find putting a nightmare, first check that your method is sufficiently accurate, then promise yourself that you will attack every putt within ten or twelve feet. This will be a positive action and build confidence. Many putts are missed through indecision, and feeble attempts to dribble or coax the ball into the hole. Be like our 1987 Open Champion, Nick Faldo, who always strokes the ball into the hole with firmness and authority.

Many poor golfers are frightened of playing with players who are better than themselves. They are often frightened of making fools of themselves. This may be a risk in other sports, but in golf we have workable handicaps. Handicaps really do work, so use your shots intelligently. Show the better player that you know how to plan your shots, and he will respect and admire you. Always take time to think and plan each shot.

Fig 62 (right) Although his playing partners don't necessarily agree, Lee Trevino believes that fooling around with the crowd makes him happy and helps his golf game.

If you fail to get out of a deep bunker, don't worry, assess the situation and if necessary play out backwards. It only costs one stroke and will save a lot of heartache.

Golfers always marvel at professionals who perform well in front of thousands of spectators and TV cameras, but it is their business. If you are faced with a large gallery, make use of them and get them on your side by smiling. When you hit a really good shot, say 'Not bad for a ? handicap player,' or 'Was that really me who hit that one?' All these things help you, and get the spectators on your side. This can be extremely useful when you play the last few holes under pressure. If the crowd are on your side they can make the difference between losing and winning.

Remember most of all, that pressure is self-inflicted. You can cause it, and you can conquer it. Smile and think clearly and positively, and you will smile and play yourself to successful golf.

19 Practising can be Fun

There are golfers who swing themselves (their body) too much, and those who swing the club (hands and arms). Players who swing their arms and hands too much should not cut this action down, but learn to use their body and legs more. Always practise the weaker links.

My stockbroker is a very interesting and clever golfer. Apart from being a good pro-am partner, he analyses every game he plays, even to the extent of noting wind conditions. He records every drive that misses the fairway, every iron shot that misses the green, and every three putt. Because of this detail he knows exactly which part of his game to practise. He's a hard man to beat on the golf course, and a good man to know in the stock-market! Practice brings its own rewards in every business.

Few high-handicap players fit into the above category. These players usually fling themselves at the ball in a determined effort to squeeze those extra yards out of the shot. The more advanced players realise that it is, in fact, only loft and clubhead speed that determine how far the ball will fly.

The best exercise to increase this speed is to select a middle iron (5 or 6) and hit dozens of balls, with the feet only a few inches apart. This develops the hand and arm action, and stops the player using the shoulders too much on the downswing. Naturally, if the shoulders move too far, without a firm foothold, the player will overbalance. Try this exercise, first by hitting chip shots, then build up to full pitch shots, finishing off with a few full swings. You will be amazed at how far you can hit the ball with your feet almost touching. It is a great exercise for learning exactly when and where to supply the *hit* or *acceleration*, during the downswing. Find out for yourself whether you should hit late or early.

A golf course is the place for enjoyment and competition. Analysing one's game and practising are not as boring as they sound. Practice should be fun, and can be a game in itself. Every shot hit on the practice ground should be aimed at a target. After hitting ten shots with a certain club, check to see how far the balls are from the target. Now move position,

Fig 63 This is the proper way to present the clubface to the golf ball. From this start, all good swings are possible.

Fig 64 This is the way so many long-handicap amateurs address the ball. The top edge of the golf club is fairly square, but the leading edge is quite closed.

Fig 65 The clubface is far too open. From this open position, a lot of compensatory movements with the hands and wrists will be necessary.

Fig 66   The clubface has too much loft on it. This is usually caused by positioning the hands too far behind the ball, or having the ball too far forward in the stance.

Fig 67   When the hands are as far forward as this, the clubface is de-lofted, which will produce a very low trajectory.

change the club for a similar number, and try to hit the next batch of ten balls even nearer. This type of practice puts some pressure on each shot and makes the player concentrate much harder, rather than aimlessly whacking balls down the practice fairway. After each practice session, take out a pitching wedge or 9-iron and chip or pitch balls to the practice flag, or your ball bag. Do not improve the lie of the balls either, just play each one as you find it – after all, you cannot improve the lie on the golf course (except in Winter Rules).

I encourage my pupils to practise together, so they can each hit one or two balls and compete against each other by trying to hit the most accurate shots. Henry Cotton, three-times Open Champion, recommends that budding professionals gamble

Fig 68 Most great players like these enjoy their practice and work hard at it. Here, Ryder Cup Captain, Tony Jacklin is helping Open Champion Nick Faldo with his bunker play.

on every practice shot to try and simulate the pressure of competing at a high level. The bet should be large enough to hurt the loser.

I believe everyone can improve his golf, and improving can be enjoyable if you find ways of practising that are not boring. Golf is a game that should be fun, and having fun on the practice ground is all a part of it. Try hitting shots with a draw then try some fades. If you find this difficult, ask the help of your local pro. Learning to control the ball with draws and fades means learning to use the golf club correctly. Knowing how the club contacts the ball and how the ball is affected by the clubface, are things that few amateurs realise or practise. Instead of shifting the feet or trying to keep the left arm straight and the head down, practise hitting the ball with the clubhead at different angles. You will quickly learn more about golf this way than by trying anything else.

The clubface can be at only one of four angles when playing golf:

1. Closed – making the ball turn to the left.
2. Open – turning the ball to the right.
3. Over-lofted – sending the ball too high.
4. De-lofted – sending the ball too low.

Every shot in golf, other than a perfect shot, is produced by one of these four angles. Due to not learning the basics early in their golf life, most players use these effects to compensate in some way for their errors in technique. The ball is a great teacher, if you know how to recognise the effects of the clubhead on the ball.

The golf swing has changed very little over the last fifty years. Harry Vardon's and Bobby Jones's swings would work now, as would Max Faulkner's. All these players had, what we call, 'classic swings'. They all had complete control of themselves, and their golf clubs. They learned to control their clubheads properly. It is no fluke that they played so well for so long. Use your practice session wisely and learn the art of control.

20   Analysing Your Game

Every long-handicap amateur can improve his scores simply by planning each shot and each hole properly. This is a luxury professionals cannot use fully. Of course the reason for this is the golfer's handicap. Every teaching professional agrees, that without improving a player's swing, the pro could cut many strokes off a long-handicap amateur's score.

Whenever I play in pro-ams, I advise my playing partners on simple things like which club to use, and which part of the green or fairway to aim at. In the excitement of competing, many high-handicap players expect to hit shots like their professional partners. We pros carry yardage books and know how far each club hits the ball, so we are never undecided on which club to use. More than ninety per cent of shots played by middle and long handicap players fall short of their intended target, simply because they are not sure of the distance and expect to hit perfect shots every time.

Naturally, a long handicap player cannot guarantee to hit the ball in the middle of the club each time. In fact, if three-quarters of their shots were only hit reasonably well, distance would be easy to judge. My advice to all middle and long handicappers is to try to assess how far each club hits the ball with an average, seventy-five per cent hit, and also estimate how far the ball carries before it hits the ground. This is important when there is a bunker or lake in front of the target. All golfers hit the ball with different trajectories so this is particularly important.

When receiving instruction from professionals who give clinics or demonstrations, most golfers do not listen to the grip part, saying, 'We know all that.' Yet so many of them get it wrong and are not prepared to change, preferring to use some gimmick to help their game.

Remember, too, that a slicer will lose more distance playing against the wind, or when it is blowing from the right-hand side. A hook will usually fly lower than a slice, so it is affected less.

It is easier to plan a hole or shot for a shorter hitter than a longer one. Most times the shorter hitter has a choice. Long hitters usually slice or hook more, so this is another reason for

Fig 69   Analysing your game: (a), always attack, as the ball cannot go down if it is short; (b) and (c), allow for your natural fade or draw in competitions, rather than trying to alter your swing during an important round.

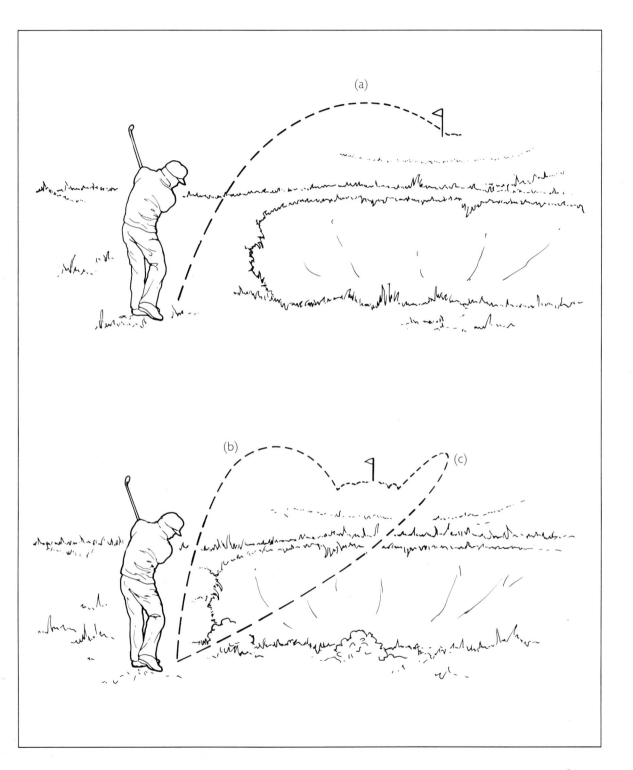

planning carefully. The reason Seve Ballesteros is such a good player is that he not only hits the ball vast distances, but he can also hook or slice with a great deal of accuracy when the occasion necessitates. We lesser mortals do not have the same choice.

When I was a young tournament pro I was sponsored by a very clever businessman who made me analyse every shot I played, whether in tournament or just in practice. Because of this, I was able to separate my strengths from my weaknesses. This was most enlightening and enabled me to make the most of my practice times. Most golfers, whether expert or beginner, blame their putting more often than any other part of their game. I am certain that if they really analysed all their shots, their views would change.

How many drives miss the fairway? How many easy iron shots miss greens? Not to mention, how many poor chip shots and how many bad risks were taken, when a safe shot would have been more sensible? All these questions can be answered if five minutes are set aside to check these things after a round.

If a player tends to slice, why not aim left a little to allow for it during the play of a round? If a hook is consistent, why fight it? Aim a little right and let it happen. The practice ground is the place for intense practice and correction.

21 The Next Step

In compiling this book I have tried to show you that most things are possible in golf instruction. If a player wishes to improve his game, whether he has a low or high handicap, attention to certain details and a little practice will ensure improvement.

It is difficult for any golfer to understand how to improve, unless certain basics are observed and the player knows why the ball spins in certain directions. It is only when a player has learned how to recognise the flight and spin of the ball that he can make genuine, lasting progress.

Any practice done without this knowledge is wholly worthless in my opinion. Although some progress can seem to be made without this essential knowledge, the improvement usually is short lived, and very inconsistent.

I know many players who have played golf for several years without this technical insight. This is because few professionals prior to about 1975 had the thorough training that young pros have today. Formerly, professionals taught personal thoughts and ideas which they had tried out with minor success, passing them on to pupils who were eager to try something new.

I cannot emphasise enough the importance of having lessons as soon as possible. So many British golfers try to learn to play by themselves and without instruction, for many months or even years, before deciding to ask for professional help. In cases like this, the pro has a real problem. Any change he recommends feels desperately uncomfortable and the player's confidence takes a knock. Most good instructors enjoy teaching beginners as they have no preconceived ideas about the golf swing. Everything the professional tells a beginner is new and exciting and is usually carried out with confidence. If any pupil puts their confidence in the instructor, improvement is immediate and usually lasting.

Learning from books, such as this one, is most useful if the player reads a passage first, thinks about it, then takes the book to the practice ground and follows the teaching, step by step. The reason for this is that most people only digest about a quarter of what they are told or read. It is better to read a

Fig 70   The cameraman should stand in this position to check swing direction, stance and aim. This is where all good professionals teach from.

Fig 71   The correct position for the
video camera, when checking the ball
position and grip.

small amount at a time so the mind can absorb the material and the brain can store it away.

As I have said, a video camera is useful for the good player – it can pick out obvious faults such as overswinging, or swings that are too flat, or too upright; it can also prove an incorrect aim, if filmed from the correct position. Nevertheless, the camera is not as good as the human eye. The trained eye can pick out far more detail than the video, particularly as one rarely sees the flight of the ball on the screen and, of course, the ball tells us everything.

I firmly believe that players can learn from each other if they know what to look for. Use this book as a reference and ask your friends to check that you really are doing what you think.

Learning can be fun – and the more a person absorbs, the more fun it is. The fun comes when the results start to show and they only happen when the message is clear in the mind and, because of this, the body starts functioning with confidence. After reading this book I certainly hope you will now go out and play better golf.

Index